C0-AVF-371

Microsoft®
PowerPoint®

Version 3

For Windows™

Step
by Step

Steve Johnson
for Perspection

Microsoft PRESS

PUBLISHED BY
Microsoft Press
A Division of Microsoft Corporation
One Microsoft Way
Redmond, Washington 98052-6399

Library of Congress Cataloging-in-Publication Data.
Johnson, Steven M., 1961-
    Microsoft Powerpoint for windows step by step / Steven M. Johnson.
        p.   cm.
    Includes index.
    ISBN 1-55615-502-6
    1. Windows (Computer programs) 2. Microsoft PowerPoint (Computer
program) I. Title.
    QA76.76.W56J65 1992
    006.6'869 -- dc20   92-14743
                                 CIP

Printed and bound in the United States of America.

1 2 3 4 5 6 7 8 9 M L M L 7 6 5 4 3 2

Distributed to the book trade in Canada by Macmillan of Canada, a division of
Canada Publishing Corporation.

Distributed to the book trade outside the United States and Canada by Penguin Books Ltd.

Penguin Books Ltd., Harmondsworth, Middlesex, England
Penguin Books Australia Ltd., Ringwood, Victoria, Australia
Penguin Books N.Z. Ltd., 182-190 Wairau Road, Auckland 10, New Zealand

British Cataloging-in-Publication Data available.

PostScript is a registered trademark of Adobe Systems, Inc. Apple, Macintosh, and TrueType are registered trademarks of Apple Computer, Inc. AutoCAD is a registered trademark of Autodesk, Inc. Genigraphics is a registered trademark and GraphicsLink is a trademark of Genigraphics Corporation. HP is a registered trademark of Hewlett-Packard Company. IBM is a registered trademark of International Business Machines Corporation. Century Schoolbook is a trademark of Kingsley-ATF Type Corporation. 1-2-3 and Lotus are registered trademarks of Lotus Development Corporation. Micrografx Designer is a trademark of Micrografx Corporation. Microsoft, MS, MS-DOS, and PowerPoint are registered trademarks and Windows and the Windows operating system logo are trademarks of Microsoft Corporation. Arial and Monotype are registered trademarks of The Monotype Corporation PLC. WordPerfect is a registered trademark of WordPerfect Corporation.

The Perspection, Inc. Publishing Group
Additional Writer: David W. Beskeen
Editor: Darvin Wilson
Graphics: Mark S. Keener
Promotion: Don Miller

Contents

Part 3 Making Your Ideas Communicate

Part 4   Adding Graphs

Part 5   Inserting and Linking Information

About This Book

Microsoft PowerPoint is the best presentation graphics program for business presenters. It is the easiest to learn and use, and delivers the highest-quality output.

Microsoft PowerPoint Step by Step is a comprehensive tutorial that shows you how to take advantage of Microsoft PowerPoint features—word processing, outlining, drawing, graphing, and presentation management tools—to create effective presentations. You can use this book in a classroom setting, or you can use it as a tutorial to learn PowerPoint at your own pace and convenience. Each lesson includes a sample presentation for you to learn and practice new skills. The sample presentations contain information about PowerPoint to simplify your work and increase your productivity.

Finding the Best Starting Point for You

This book is designed for both new users learning PowerPoint for the first time and experienced users who want to learn to use the new features in PowerPoint version 3. If you are familiar with Microsoft PowerPoint version 2.0 for Windows or the Apple Macintosh, you'll have a head start on the basics of PowerPoint for Windows version 3. Among the new features you'll want to learn about are the Toolbar buttons, which carry out common commands with a click of the mouse, the Outline view, which enables you to outline and arrange your ideas to create a presentation, and the PowerPoint Viewer, which is a separate program that allows you to share your presentations with others without installing PowerPoint.

The modular design of this book offers you considerable flexibility in customizing your learning. Lessons 1 and 2 teach basic skills; Lessons 3 through 15 teach advanced skills. To decide if you need to work through a lesson, look at the summary at the end of the lesson. If you are unsure about any of the summary topics, work through the appropriate section of the lesson. You can go through the lessons in any order, skip lessons, and repeat lessons later to brush up on certain skills. Each lesson builds on concepts presented in previous lessons, so you might want to review an earlier lesson if you don't understand the concepts or terminology presented in a particular lesson.

You start most lessons by opening a practice file from the accompanying Practice Files disk. You then rename the practice file so that the original file remains unchanged while you work on your own version. If you make a mistake in your presentation, you can simply start that lesson over. You don't need to complete a lesson in order to go on to the next one.

The following table recommends starting points based on your presentation graphics software experience.

If you are	Follow these steps
New to Microsoft Windows	Read "Getting Ready" later in this book. Next, work through Lesson 1. Work through the other lessons in any order.
New to the mouse	Read "If You Are New to Using the Mouse" in the Getting Ready section. Next, work through Lesson 1. Work through the other lessons in any order.
New to presentation graphics	Read "Getting to Know PowerPoint" and "If You Are New to Presentation Graphics" in the Getting Ready section. Next, work through Lesson 1. Work through the other lessons in any order.
Familiar with PowerPoint version 2.0 for Windows	Read the summaries at the end of Lessons 1 and 2. Next, read Appendix C, "New Features of Microsoft PowerPoint." Complete the lessons that best meet your needs.

Using This Book as a Classroom Aid

If you're an instructor, you can use *Microsoft PowerPoint Step by Step* to teach novice users about PowerPoint or teach experienced users about PowerPoint's new features. You can also choose from the lessons to customize courses for your students.

If you plan to teach the entire contents of this book, you should probably set aside two days of classroom time to allow for discussion, questions, and any customized practice you might wish to create.

Conventions Used in This Book

Before you start any of the lessons, it's important that you understand the terms and step by step conventions used in this book.

Step by Step Conventions

- Numbered lists (1, 2, 3, and so on) indicate a sequence of steps you are to follow. A triangular bullet (▶) indicates a procedure with only one step.

- The word *choose* instructs you to carry out a command.

- The word *select* instructs you to highlight objects, or text, and to select options in a dialog box.

- Characters you are to type appear in **bold.**

- Important terms and titles of books appear in *italic*.

Keyboard Conventions

- Names of keys are in small capital letters (for example, TAB and SHIFT).

- A plus sign (+) between two key names means that you must press those keys at the same time. For example, "Press SHIFT+SPACEBAR" means that you hold down the SHIFT key while you press the SPACEBAR.

Other Features of this Book

Outline View

- Many commands can be carried out by clicking a button on the Toolbar or Tool Palette. If a procedure instructs you to click a button, a picture of the button appears in the left margin, as it does here for the Outline View button.

- Text in the left margin summarizes main points, or gives additional useful information.

- You'll find optional "One Step Further" exercises at the end of the lessons. These exercises are less structured than the lessons to help you practice what you learned in the lessons.

TROUBLESHOOTING: **If you get unexpected results as you work**   If what happens on the screen is not what you expected, look for a Troubleshooting note below the step where the problem occurred. Troubleshooting notes are marked in the left margin, as shown here.

Cross-References to Microsoft PowerPoint Documentation

Microsoft PowerPoint Step by Step and your Microsoft PowerPoint documentation are a powerful combination to help you learn the product. At the end of every lesson is a listing of topics covered and where to find them in your *Microsoft PowerPoint Handbook*. Marginal notes in the text of the lesson also direct you to more information. Using the references to these sources will help you to make greater use of Microsoft PowerPoint's powerful features.

Microsoft PowerPoint Handbook   The handbook is the single book with all the information you need to operate Microsoft PowerPoint. Each chapter describes a particular task and explains the procedures you follow to accomplish that task.

Using Microsoft PowerPoint and Genigraphics Presentation Services   This booklet shows you how to create 35mm slides using the Genigraphics driver and how to send your file using the GeniLink.

Presentations on the Go   This booklet shows you how to create presentations on a notebook computer while traveling.

What's New in Microsoft PowerPoint   This booklet describes what's new in PowerPoint version 3 and the differences from PowerPoint version 2.0. This booklet includes menu and feature changes, and installation suggestions. For a list of the new features, along with the lesson in this book in which you can learn about each feature, see Appendix C, "New Features of Microsoft PowerPoint."

Online Help   You can get Help on your screen by pressing F1 or by choosing a command from the Help menu. Within Help, you can set bookmarks, search for specific topics by keyboard, and print Help text.

Templates   PowerPoint comes with a set of formatted templates you can use to produce different kinds of presentations, including black and white overheads, color overheads, 35mm slides, and on-screen electronic presentations.

Clip Art   With Clip Art you can paste ready-made graphics directly into PowerPoint presentations, and edit them to meet your specific needs. These graphics are available by choosing Open Clip Art from the File menu.

Timesavers   These are common diagrams such as organizational charts, calendars, tables, timelines, and flowcharts that are ready to cut and paste into your PowerPoint presentations. These PowerPoint presentations are stored in the TIMESAVR subdirectory and can be accessed by choosing the Open command from the File menu.

Building a Quick-Reference Notebook

The sample presentations you'll use along with the lessons contain useful quick-reference information about Microsoft PowerPoint. If you print these sample presentations at the end of each lesson, you can build a quick-reference notebook of helpful tips and techniques you can use later to help you create other presentations.

Getting Ready

This book shows how you can easily create business presentations by using the features in Microsoft PowerPoint. Each lesson takes approximately 20 to 50 minutes, including the optional One Step Further sections at the end of each lesson. Before you begin the lessons, this portion of the book shows you how to install the practice files on your computer's hard drive, explains how to start Windows 3.1, and introduces you to Microsoft PowerPoint.

If you have not yet installed Windows 3.1 or PowerPoint version 3, you'll need to do that before you continue with the lessons. For instructions on installing Windows version 3.1, see your Windows documentation. Instructions for installing Microsoft PowerPoint for Windows can be found in Appendix A, "Installing Microsoft PowerPoint," or your Microsoft PowerPoint for Windows documentation.

Installing the Step by Step Practice Files

At the back of this book you'll find a disk named "Microsoft PowerPoint Step by Step Practice Files." A special program on the disk will copy the practice files onto your hard drive for you.

Set up the practice files on your hard disk

1   Insert the Microsoft PowerPoint Step by Step practice files disk into drive A (or B) of your computer.

2   At the system prompt (usually "C:\"), either type **a:install** or **b:install** depending on the drive you use, and then press ENTER.

3   Follow the instructions on the screen. You can press CTRL+X at any time to exit the Step by Step setup program.

The Step by Step setup program displays a message asking where you want to install the practice files. The program copies the files from the floppy disk into the directory that you specify and stores them in a subdirectory called PRACTICE. Remember the name of the drive and directory where the practice files are stored so you can open the files for each lesson. It's best to place the PRACTICE subdirectory in the directory that contains the Microsoft PowerPoint for Windows program. This is normally the POWERPNT directory.

Later, as you work through the lessons, be sure to follow the instructions for renaming the practice files so that you can go through a lesson more than once if you wish.

For a complete list of the practice files and the lessons in which they are used, see Appendix E, "List of Practice Files."

Starting PowerPoint

After you have installed Microsoft PowerPoint and the practice files, you can start PowerPoint from the system prompt, or you can start PowerPoint from within Windows.

Starting PowerPoint from the System Prompt

1   At the system prompt (usually C:\), change to the directory that contains PowerPoint for Windows by typing **cd** *directory name*

2   Type **win powerpnt**

3   Press ENTER.

Proceed to the section "Getting to Know PowerPoint."

Starting PowerPoint from within Windows

Use the following procedure to start Microsoft Windows and Microsoft PowerPoint, and to familiarize yourself with the Windows Program Manager. The appearance of your screen might be different from the illustrations that follow, depending on your particular setup. For more information about Windows 3.1, see your Windows 3.1 documentation.

Start Windows

1   At the system prompt, type **win**

2   Press ENTER.

When you start Windows, the Program Manager window is displayed. You can start all of your applications, including Microsoft PowerPoint for Windows, from the Program Manager.

Microsoft PowerPoint group

While Windows is active, everything on your screen displays in a *window*. You can make each window any size you want and move it anywhere you want on your screen. You can have multiple windows open at the same time.

The Program Manager   Within the Program Manager window are several *icons*. The icons in the Program Manager window organize applications into groups so that you can easily find them. Opening a group in the Program Manager reveals another window of related applications and documents.

The Microsoft PowerPoint group   Double-clicking the Microsoft PowerPoint group icon opens another window, which contains icons for Microsoft PowerPoint, PowerPoint Viewer, and GraphicsLink applications.

Start Microsoft PowerPoint for Windows

1   Double-click the Microsoft PowerPoint group icon.

The Microsoft PowerPoint group opens.

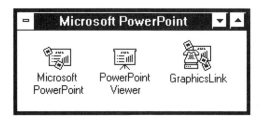

2   Double-click the Microsoft PowerPoint icon.

Getting to Know PowerPoint

When you start Microsoft PowerPoint, a new *presentation window* appears. The presentation window is PowerPoint's equivalent of a presentation slide. It is your canvas on which to type text, draw shapes, and create graphs. The buttons you see at the top of the window on the *Toolbar* are the tools you need to work on your presentations. The buttons on the *Tool Palette* at the left side of the window are the drawing tools you need to communicate your ideas and create graphs. At the bottom of the window are view buttons you use to switch to different PowerPoint views.

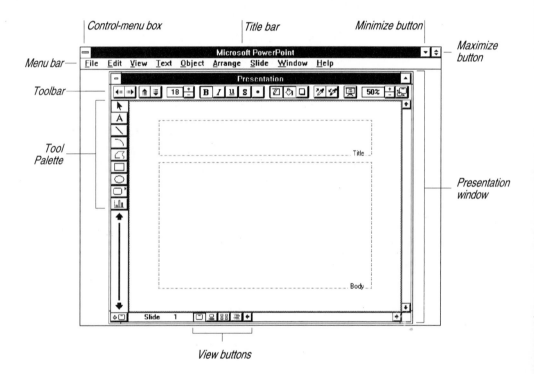

You can adjust the size of the PowerPoint window with the Minimize or Maximize buttons. You can also click and drag the Title bar to move the Microsoft PowerPoint or presentation windows. With the Control-menu box, you can close or restore the PowerPoint window, or switch to another Windows-based application.

PowerPoint Views

PowerPoint gives you four views to create and organize your presentation. Slide view allows you to work on individual slides. Notes view allows you to create speaker's notes. Slide Sorter view shows you a miniature of each slide in your presentation. Outline view allows you to work with all the title and body text in your presentation. You can switch between views with the buttons at the bottom of the presentation window. An example of each presentation window is shown below.

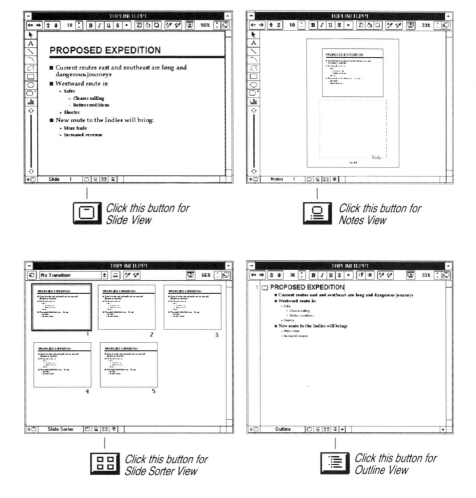

Click this button for Slide View

Click this button for Notes View

Click this button for Slide Sorter View

Click this button for Outline View

PowerPoint Toolbar

Across the top of the presentation window, PowerPoint's Toolbar offers shortcuts to commonly used commands for outlining, formatting text, and changing object styles. PowerPoint uses three different Toolbars, as illustrated below.

Toolbar in Slide view and Notes view

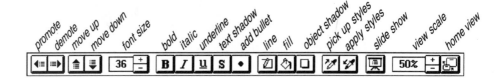

Toolbar in Outline view

Toolbar in Slide Sorter view

PowerPoint Tool Palette

PowerPoint comes with a powerful set of tools for drawing, graphing, and adding text to your slides. These tools are on the Tool Palette located on the left side of the presentation window.

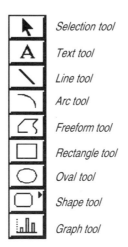

Selection tool

Text tool

Line tool

Arc tool

Freeform tool

Rectangle tool

Oval tool

Shape tool

Graph tool

If You Are New to Presentation Graphics

Each time you start PowerPoint, you either create a new presentation or work on a presentation that you or someone else has already created. You create a presentation in a series of steps, as shown below.

Step 1   Enter your ideas

PowerPoint opens a presentation ready for you to enter your ideas. Concentrate on entering your ideas first and formatting them later. Type in a title and some supporting information on a slide or in the outliner, incorporate slides from other presentations, or import outlines from other applications such as Word for Windows.

Step 2   Edit and arrange your content

Refine your content by editing and rearranging text in Outline and Slide views, and by moving slides around in the Slide Sorter view.

Step 3   Format your presentation for a consistent look

As you refine your content, you can start formatting your presentation to give it a professional, consistent look. If you apply a template to your presentation, PowerPoint formats your content to match the template format. You can also format text and graphical objects individually.

Step 4   Add clip art, graphics, and charts

PowerPoint makes it easy to communicate your ideas with graphical images. Over 500 clip art images come with PowerPoint. The Shape tool allows you to click and drag to draw one of 24 different shapes. You can also import graphical images from other applications, like Microsoft Excel.

Step 5   Enter notes and create handout pages

Along with your presentation slides, you can create speaker's notes pages and audience handouts to complete your presentation with PowerPoint.

Step 6   Print your slides, notes, handouts, and outline pages

You'll have opportunities to print presentations during these lessons. If you're unable to print your presentation, or if your presentation prints on a different printer than you expected, read through Appendix B, "Installing and Selecting a Printer."

If You Are New to Using the Mouse

Toolbars, shortcut menus, and many other features of Microsoft PowerPoint were designed for working with the mouse. Though you can use the keyboard for some actions, many of these actions are easier to do with the mouse.

Mouse Pointers

The mouse controls a pointer on the screen. You can move the pointer by sliding the mouse over a flat surface in the direction you want the pointer on the screen to move. If you run out of room on your flat surface to move the mouse, lift it and then put it down where there is still room to move. The pointer doesn't move while the mouse is not touching the flat surface.

Moving the pointer across the screen by moving the mouse does not affect the presentation; the pointer simply indicates a location on the screen. When you press the mouse button while moving the mouse or positioning the pointer on certain screen objects, you can perform a variety of operations.

When the pointer passes over certain parts of the Presentation window, it changes shape to indicate what it does at that position. The following pointer shapes appear during the lessons.

Pointer shape	Significance
⌖	This pointer, known as the "pointer," appears after you select the Selection Tool button from the Tool Palette. With it you can select any object by clicking the object itself or by clicking on a blank area and dragging the pointer across the object, which creates a *selection box*.

Pointer shape	Significance
	This pointer, known as the "text cursor," appears after you select the Text Tool button from the Tool Palette. Use this pointer to create text objects.
	This pointer, known as the "cross hairs cursor," appears after you select a drawing tool from the Tool Palette. Click in a blank area and drag to create a box for a drawing, a line, or a graph.
	This pointer, known as the "I-beam cursor," appears after you select a text object or a shape that includes text. Use this pointer to indicate where you want to begin typing or select and edit text.
	This pointer, known as the "four-headed arrow," appears when you move the pointer over a bullet or slide icon in Outline view or a bullet in Slide view.

Using the Mouse

Moving the mouse and pressing the mouse button are the only skills necessary to master the basic skills of *pointing*, *clicking*, *double-clicking*, and *dragging*. These are the four basic mouse actions that you use throughout these lessons.

Pointing   Moving the mouse to place the pointer on an item is called *pointing*.

Clicking   Pointing to an item on your screen and then quickly pressing and releasing the mouse button is called *clicking*.

Double-clicking   Pointing to an item and quickly pressing and releasing the mouse button twice is called *double-clicking*. This is a convenient shortcut for many of the tasks you'll perform in PowerPoint.

Dragging   Holding down the mouse button as you move the pointer is called *dragging*. You can use this technique to move text and objects and perform other important tasks.

For all instructions that call for clicking, double-clicking, and dragging, always use the left mouse button unless you've made changes in the Windows Control Panel.

If You Are New to Using Commands and Dialog Boxes

A *command* is an instruction to PowerPoint to perform an action such as copying text, making text bold, or printing a presentation. PowerPoint commands are grouped together in *menus* and *submenus*. The buttons on the Toolbar provide quick access to the most frequently used commands in PowerPoint. All of the commands in PowerPoint, including those on the Toolbar, are available by opening menus on the menu bar.

Choosing Menu Commands

You can choose commands in PowerPoint by using the mouse or the keyboard. This book assumes you are using a mouse to choose commands.

Choosing a command with the mouse

To choose a command with the mouse, click the menu name and then choose the command. If a command leads to a submenu, an additional menu of more choices appears when you choose the command. If a submenu appears, click another command from the list that appears. To cancel a menu without choosing a command, click outside of the menu or press ALT.

Choosing a command with the keyboard

To choose a command with the keyboard, press ALT to activate the menu bar and then press the key that corresponds with the underlined letter of the menu you want to open. For example, to choose the Open command from the File menu, press ALT, F, O. If you press ALT and then want to cancel the command, press ALT again. You can also carry out some commands with the keyboard shortcuts shown in the menu.

Menu Conventions

PowerPoint menus follow certain conventions. If you click a menu name, you'll see commands with keyboard shortcuts, submenus, and ellipses (...), as well as some dimmed commands.

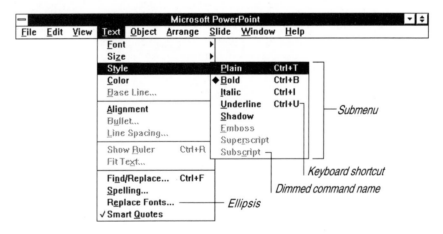

Keyboard shortcuts   Some menu commands list shortcut key combinations to the right of the command name. For example, CTRL+U is the keyboard shortcut for the Underline command. As you become familiar with menus and commands, these shortcut keys can save you time.

Submenus   When you choose a command name with a black arrow to the right of the command name, a *submenu* opens with more command choices.

Ellipses   When you choose a command name followed by an ellipsis (...), PowerPoint displays a dialog box so that you can provide more information. The dialog box prompts you to enter information, or choose from a list of options. For example, the Open command on the File menu is followed by an ellipsis because you need to tell PowerPoint which presentation you want to open.

Command name dimmed   When a command name appears dimmed, it doesn't apply to your current situation or is unavailable. For example, the Subscript command appears dimmed in the previous illustration because no text has been selected to change to subscript text style.

PowerPoint menu conventions

Some PowerPoint menus contain command settings that indicate status. These settings appear on menus in several ways.

Diamond

Diamond   A diamond indicates a default setting. For example, the Style command on the Text menu uses Bold as a default setting.

Bullet

Bullet   A bullet indicates an existing choice for a selected object, a chosen view, or an option in a dialog box.

Checkmark

Checkmark   A checkmark indicates that a feature is turned on. For example, the Smart Quotes command on the Text menu uses the checkmark to indicate the feature is turned on. If Smart Quotes is turned off, the checkmark does not appear.

Using Dialog Boxes

For many commands, PowerPoint displays a dialog box in which you select options that specify how the command should be carried out. Dialog boxes vary according to what kind of information you need to provide. Many have certain features in common, such as check boxes, lists, and command buttons.

Choose a command

When you choose a command name followed by an ellipsis (...), PowerPoint displays a dialog box. For example, the Open dialog box displays when you choose the Open command from the File menu.

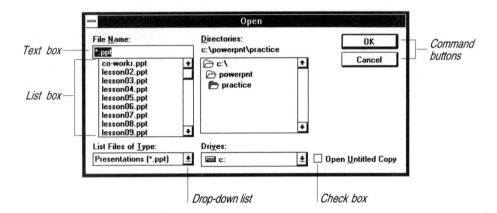

Select options using check boxes

Dialog boxes often include check boxes to select options that are independent of one another, so you can select more than one at a time. For example, in the dialog box shown above, an "X" in the box next to Open Untitled Copy indicates the option is turned on.

Select options using option buttons

When a dialog box includes option buttons, you can select only one option at a time from a group of option buttons. For example, in the Print dialog box, you can select the All, Current Slide, or Slides option button. A selected option button has a black dot in its center.

Select options from a list

When several alternatives are available for an option, they are frequently indicated by a drop-down list. You can display the list by clicking the down arrow.

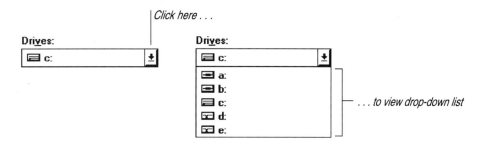

Type information in a text box

For some dialog boxes you must type specific information in a text box to complete the command. For example, in the Find/Replace dialog box you must type in the text you would like to find before you can click the Find button to complete the command.

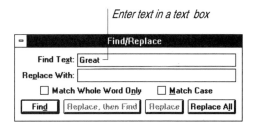

Get Help about dialog box options

When you are working in a dialog box, you can read about the options by pressing the F1 key. PowerPoint displays a Help window that describes the command and the dialog box options.

Complete the command

For most dialog boxes, to complete the command and execute the instructions, click the OK button. Conversely, to cancel your instructions in a dialog box, click the Cancel button.

Troubleshooting Guide

If you open the wrong lesson presentation, or if you cannot find the PRACTICE subdirectory, the lesson directs you to this troubleshooting section. You do not need to work through this section now; simply refer to it as you need to while working through the lessons.

Displaying the List of Practice Files

You begin most of the lessons by opening one of the sample presentations available on the Practice Files disk. The practice files should already be stored on your hard drive in a subdirectory called PRACTICE. If they are not, see "Installing the Step by Step Practice Files," beginning on page xiii. After the files are copied onto your hard drive, you can select them by doing the following:

1 From the File menu, choose Open.

Choosing the Open command displays the Open dialog box, in which you select the name of the presentation you want to open.

2 If the box under "Drives" does not display the drive where the practice files are stored, click the down arrow next to the box and choose the name of the correct drive from the drop-down list. For most users, this is drive C.

3 In the box under "Directories," find the name of the directory where the PRACTICE subdirectory is stored. The POWERPNT directory is a likely location for the PRACTICE subdirectory. You might need to click the up or down arrow next to the box to see all the directories in the list. When you find the name of the directory, double-click on it to open the directory and display the PRACTICE subdirectory.

4 Double-click the PRACTICE subdirectory. The box under "File Name" lists the name of the practice files. Click the up or down arrow next to the box to see the names of all the practice files.

You are now ready to open a file. Return to the lesson to get the name of the file you need and then continue. Open the file by clicking the file name and then the OK button, or by double-clicking the file name.

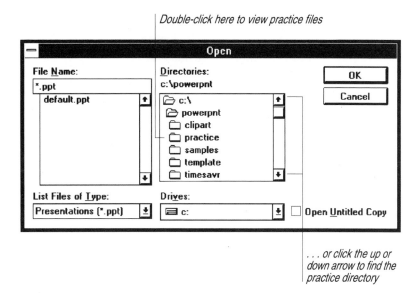

Double-click here to view practice files

. . . or click the up or down arrow to find the practice directory

Changing Your Screen Display to Match the Illustrations

If you share your computer with others, previous users might have changed the screen setup. You can easily change it back so that the screen matches the illustrations in the lesson. Use the following methods to control the screen display.

If you are in a different view

If you're viewing your presentation in a different view than the one indicated in the text, you can easily change it by clicking the view buttons at the bottom of the presentation window.

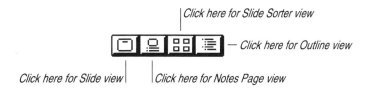

Click here for Slide Sorter view

— Click here for Outline view

Click here for Slide view

Click here for Notes Page view

If PowerPoint does not fill the screen

If the PowerPoint window doesn't fill the screen, you can enlarge the window by clicking the Maximize button to the far right of the Microsoft PowerPoint Title bar.

Maximize button

If an object or text seems unusually large or small

To increase or decrease the view scale of your presentation, click the (+) or (-) View Scale buttons on the Toolbar.

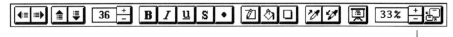

Click the + button or the - button to change view scale

Part

Learning Microsoft PowerPoint Basics

Creating a New Presentation

With Microsoft PowerPoint you can create slides, speaker's notes, audience handouts, and an outline, all in a single presentation file. In this lesson, you'll learn to enter and rearrange your ideas and format text. You'll type title and body text, create new slides, look at your content in different views, and move around your presentation. At the end of the lesson, your presentation will consist of the following slides:

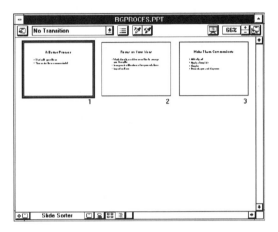

This lesson explains how to do the following:

- Type title and body text on a slide
- Create a new slide
- Change presentation views
- Move from slide to slide
- Preview slides
- Name and save your presentation for future use
- End your PowerPoint session

Estimated lesson time: 35 minutes

The Presentation Window

*If you haven't started
PowerPoint yet, first
work through
"Getting Ready,"
beginning on page
xiii.*

When you start PowerPoint, the basic PowerPoint window appears, with a new presentation opened. The new presentation window includes an empty slide, which is your canvas to type text, draw graphics, and create graphs. The presentation view can be changed to the notes page for entering speaker notes, the slide sorter for arranging slides, and the outliner for organizing text.

Along the top of the presentation window are the tools and features you'll use to do most of your text and object handling tasks. The new Toolbar makes common tasks easy. Simply click on the Toolbar for one-step access to tasks such as formatting text, adding frames and shadows to objects, and changing view scales.

At the left of the presentation window on the Tool Palette are the tools you'll use to draw objects and freeform shapes, create word-processing and label text, and create two-dimensional and three-dimensional graphs.

At the bottom of the presentation window are view buttons that allow you to look at your presentation in different ways—Slide, Notes, Slide Sorter, and Outline views, as well as, the New Slide button and the View Status box.

Inside the presentation window are two text boxes. The one at the top is a placeholder for the slide's title, and is called the *Title Object*. The lower box is for the slide's body text, and is called the *Body Object*. Each slide contains a Title object and a Body object unless you delete them.

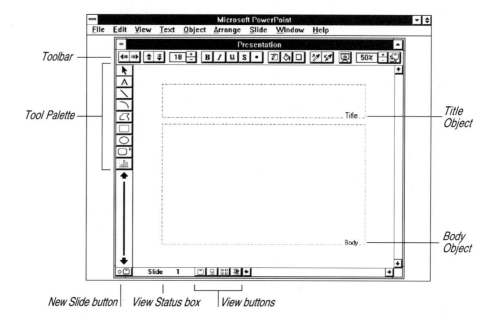

Entering Text in Slide View

If you are new to Presentation Graphics, see "Getting Ready," earlier in this book.

Throughout this book, text that you are to type appears in bold.

Type title and body text in Slide view

To give your slide a title, click on the Title object, and start typing. If you make a mistake as you type, press the BACKSPACE key to delete the mistake, and then type the correct text.

1   Click the Title object and type **A Better Process**

The object is surrounded by a "fuzzy" outline called a *selection box* to indicate the object is selected.

2   Click the Body object to select it.

The Title object is deselected.

3   Type **Start with your ideas** and press ENTER.

Bullets appear before each body point by default.

4   Type **Then make them communicate!**

Your presentation window should look similar to the following illustration:

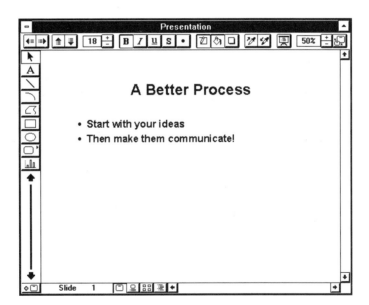

Creating a New Slide in Slide View

You can create a new slide in any view in your presentation using either the New Slide button or the New Slide command from the Slide menu.

New Slide

▶ Click the New Slide button in the lower-left corner of the window.

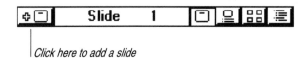

| Click here to add a slide

A new empty slide is added after the current slide in Slide view. The View Status box displays slide 2.

Enter text in a new slide

If you start typing on an empty slide with nothing selected, PowerPoint enters the text into the Title object.

▶ Type **Focus on Your Ideas**

PowerPoint lets you work directly in Slide view or Outline view to enter your ideas. Let's change views and complete this slide in Outline view.

Changing Views

The View buttons at the bottom of the presentation window let you view or work on your presentation in different ways—Slide view, Outline view, Slide Sorter view, and Notes view. These view commands are also available on the View menu.

Change to Outline view

You'll continue to enter your ideas in Outline view. The Outline view shows your presentation in the form of an outline. From the Slide view, change to Outline view.

Outline View

▶ Click the Outline View button.

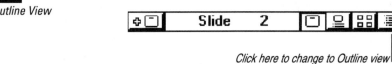

Click here to change to Outline view|

A slide icon appears to the left of each slide's title. Body text underneath each title appears indented one level with bullets. The title from slide 2 is selected as shown in the following illustration:

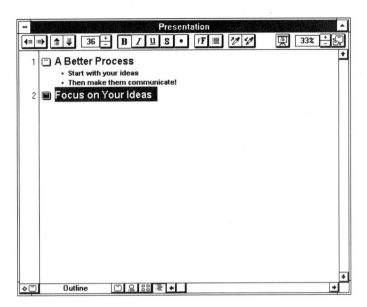

TROUBLESHOOTING: **If your screen doesn't look the same**   Check your current view. If you're in a different view, click the Outline view button. If you accidently double-click a view button, PowerPoint changes to a master view. If this happens, click the appropriate view button again. To check which view your presentation is in, check the View Status box to the left of the view buttons.

Changing View Scale

You can change the scale of your view by using the View Scale buttons on the Toolbar or the View menu. The view scales available are 25%, 33%, 50%, 66%, Actual size (100%), 200%, and 400%.

View Scale

1   On the Toolbar, click the View Scale (+) button.

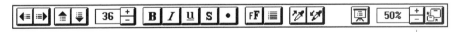

Click the + button or the - button to change view scale to 50%

The view scale size increases from 33% to 50%. The View Scale buttons allow you to increase the view scale to see smaller text or decrease the view scale to see more of the presentation.

Home Scale

2   On the Toolbar, click the Home Scale button.

Click here to change to Home Scale view

The Home Scale button toggles between the home scale for the current view—Slide, Notes, Slide Sorter, Outline—and the view scale of your choice. The view scale size changes to 33%, which is the home scale for Outline view.

Entering Text in Outline View

To enter text in Outline view, position the insertion point where you want text to start or choose New Slide from the Slide menu and begin typing. Adding a new slide in Outline view creates a new slide icon. If you want to add body text to the previous slide, use the Demote button on the Toolbar or the TAB key.

Create a new slide and enter text

In this section, you'll create a new slide, change the indent level and type in body text to complete slide 2. If you make a mistake as you type, press the BACKSPACE key to delete the mistake, and then type the correct text.

New Slide

1   Click the New Slide button.

The slide icon for slide 3 appears with the insertion point flashing.

Demote

2   On the Toolbar, click the Demote button.

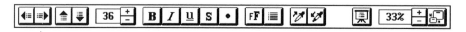

Click here to demote slides and text

The Demote button indents your text to the right one level. The slide icon changes to a small bullet. The new text for this bullet becomes the body text for slide 2.

3   Type **Work directly on slides or outline to arrange your thoughts** and press ENTER.

The cursor remains at the same indented level.

4   Type **Incorporate slides from other presentations** and press ENTER.

5   Type **Import outlines**

Create a new slide using the keyboard

With the insertion point after the word "outlines," create a new slide from an indented outline level using a keyboard command.

1 Hold down the CTRL key and press ENTER.

A new slide is created with the insertion point to the left of the slide icon. Type in another title and body text.

2 Type **Make Them Communicate** and press ENTER.

3 Press TAB.

The current slide title is indented a level to become body text for the previous slide.

4 Type **Add clip art** and press ENTER.

5 Type **Apply a template** and press ENTER.

6 Type **Add graphs** and press ENTER.

7 Type **Draw shapes and diagrams**

Insert new text

You can easily insert new text anywhere in Outline view and in Slide view.

1 Position the I-beam cursor just after the word "template" and click.

This places the blinking insertion point where you are to begin typing, as shown in the following illustration:

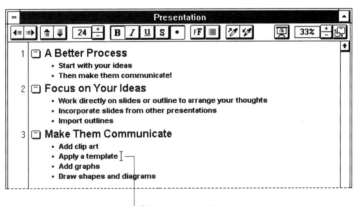

Click here to position
I-beam for text insertion

TROUBLESHOOTING: **If the insertion point is not where you want it**   Reposition the I-beam cursor and click again to place the insertion point in the desired location.

2 Press the SPACEBAR and type **for a consistent look**

PowerPoint makes room in the outline for the new text.

Select and replace text

You can select individual characters, sentences, body text, or title text in either Outline or Slide view. Selecting text in PowerPoint works just as it does in Microsoft Word for Windows.

1   Position the I-beam cursor over any part of the word "consistent" in the second bullet point of slide 3.

2   Double-click to select the word.

Your presentation window should look similar to the following illustration:

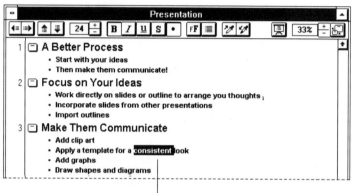

Double-click here to select text

The text is now highlighted indicating it has been selected. When you double-click a word, PowerPoint also selects the space that follows. This maintains correct spacing if you delete a word. Once you've selected text, the next text you type—regardless of its length—replaces the selection.

3   Type **professional**

The text in the outline moves over to fill the space.

Change your mind

A handy feature in PowerPoint is the Undo command (CTRL+Z), which reverses your last action. For example, choosing the Undo command now will put back into your presentation the word that you just replaced. (Whenever something happens that is confusing or is not what you intended, choose Undo as the *next* action.)

▶   From the Edit menu, choose Undo to reverse your last action.

If this does not put the original word back in the outline, you might have pressed another key before you chose the Undo command. Undo reverses only the last action that you took.

Select and rearrange text

You can easily select and rearrange individual or groups of title or body text in Outline and Slide views. In Outline view, you can also select an entire slide or groups of slides to move.

1   Move your pointer over the second bullet in slide 3.

The pointer changes to a four-headed arrow.

2   Click the bullet to select the entire line.

An entire slide can be selected by moving the pointer over the slide icon and clicking once.

Move Up

3   On the Toolbar, click the Move Up button.

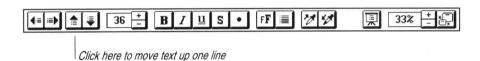

Click here to move text up one line

The entire line moves up one level.

TROUBLESHOOTING: **If you move the text past the top of the outline**   Moving a body paragraph above the top of the outline creates new slides. Press the BACKSPACE key to delete the slides.

Tip   A line of text doesn't need to be selected to be moved. Placing the insertion point anywhere in a line of text and clicking any of the Outlining buttons, the last four buttons on the left hand side of the Toolbar, will move the line of text one level.

Change to a different slide in Slide view

You can change back to Slide view and look at the slide you just created in your outline. In Slide view, you can see how the Title and Body objects appear on the slide.

1   Position the cursor over the slide icon for slide 3.

The cursor changes from the I-beam cursor to a four-headed arrow.

2   Double-click the slide icon.

Slide 3 appears in Slide view.

Tip   Double-clicking the slide number in Outline view also takes you back to the selected slide in Slide view.

Moving from Slide to Slide with the Slide Changer

Slide Changer

The Slide Changer, located in the lower-left area of the presentation window, works like a scroll bar. Drag the lever to move ahead or back more than one slide at a time. You can also click the down arrow on the Slide Changer to view the next slide or click the up arrow to view the previous slide. Use the Slide Changer to move among the slides while in Slide view or notes while in Notes view.

Move from slide to slide

▶ Click the up arrow on the Slide Changer to view the previous slide.

Your presentation window should look similar to the following illustration:

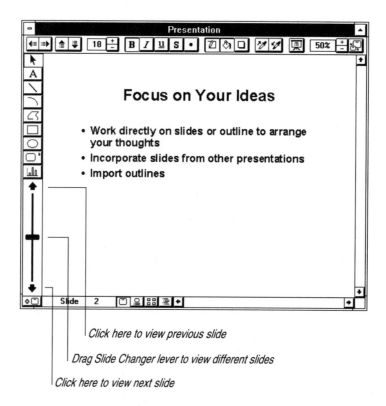

Click here to view previous slide

Drag Slide Changer lever to view different slides

Click here to view next slide

The View Status box changes from slide 3 to slide 2, and the Slide Changer lever changes position to the middle. The Slide Changer lever indicates the relative position of the slide in the presentation. Clicking above or below the Slide Changer lever also moves the slides. In Slide or Notes view, the PAGE UP key changes the view to the previous slide and the PAGE DOWN key changes the view to the next slide.

Previewing Slides in Slide Sorter View

Another way to view your presentation is to use the Slide Sorter view. The Slide Sorter view allows you to preview your presentation as if you were looking at slides on a light board. In this view—as well as in Outline view—you can easily rearrange the order of the slides in your presentation.

Change to Slide Sorter view

Slide Sorter View

▶ Click the Slide Sorter View button at the bottom of the window.

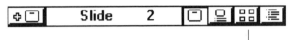

Click here to change to Slide Sorter view

All the slides now appear in miniature on the screen, and the slide you were viewing in Slide view is selected. Your presentation window should look similar to the following illustration:

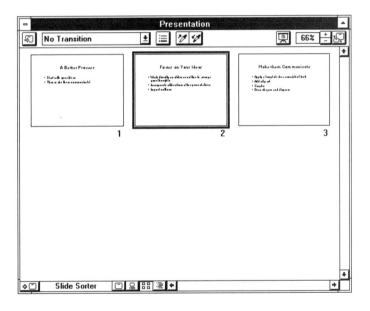

Change to a specific slide in Slide view

1   Position your pointer over slide 1.

2   Double-click slide 1.

The presentation view changes to Slide view showing slide 1.

Saving a Presentation

The work you've done is currently stored only in the computer's memory. To save the work for further use, you must give the presentation a name and store it on your hard drive.

Use the following procedure to save the presentation in the same directory as the Step by Step practice files. During the procedure, PowerPoint displays a *dialog box.* Dialog boxes supply PowerPoint with more information about what you want to do.

To choose a command, click the menu name at the top of the window, and then select the name of the command from the menu that appears.

1   Click the word "File" on the menu bar at the top of the PowerPoint window.

PowerPoint opens the File menu.

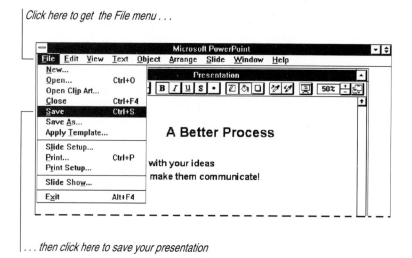

2   Choose the Save command by selecting it.

Note   In the remainder of this book, the procedure for choosing a menu command will be shortened to read "From the File menu, choose Save."

PowerPoint displays a dialog box. The insertion point is positioned in the box under the label File Name, so you can type a name for the presentation.

Document names can be no more than eight characters long. They cannot have any spaces in them.

3 Type your initials, with no periods or spaces, followed by the word **proces**

For example, if your initials are B. G., type the following without any spaces: **bgproces**

In later lessons, we'll write this instruction as "Type *your initials***proces**"

4 In the box under "Drives," check to be sure that drive C is selected (if that is where you stored your Step by Step practice files). If you need assistance, see the "Getting Ready" section earlier in this book.

5 In the list under "Directories," check to be sure that the PRACTICE directory is open. If it is not, select it by double-clicking it.

6 To close the dialog box and have PowerPoint save the presentation the way you've specified, click the OK button or press ENTER.

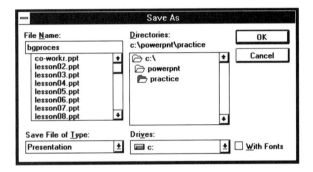

The Title bar name changes from "Presentation" to "BGPROCES.PPT"

One Step Further

You have learned two ways to enter your ideas into your PowerPoint presentation. In addition, you have learned how to enter and arrange title and body text in Slide and Outline views, how to switch between views, and how to move from slide to slide. If you'd like to practice these and other basic skills in your practice presentation, try the following:

▶ Create some new slides with the Slide button under the Slide Changer or with the menu command located in the Slide menu, and enter title and body text.

▶ Change to the Outline view and enter text. Use the Outlining buttons and keyboard commands to create new title and body text.

▶ Change to Slide view and move from slide to slide with the Slide Changer.

If you want to continue to the next lesson

1 From the File menu, choose Close (CTRL+F4).

2 If a dialog box appears asking if you want to save the changes to your presentation, click the No button.

Choosing this command closes the active presentation; it does not exit PowerPoint. If no other presentations are open, the menu bar displays two available menus: File and Help.

If you want to quit PowerPoint for now

1   From the File menu, choose Exit (ALT+F4).

2   If a dialog box appears asking if you want to save changes to the presentation, click the No button.

Lesson Summary

To	Do this
Type title and body text on a slide	Select the Title or Body object and then start typing.
Create a new slide	Click the New Slide button or from the Slide menu, choose New Slide.
Change presentation views	Click any of the view buttons: Slide, Notes, Handout, and Slide Sorter views.
Type title text in an outline	Position the insertion point to the right of a slide icon and type.
Type body text in an outline	Position the insertion point to the right of a slide icon, press TAB and type.
Move from slide to slide	Click the Slide Changer in Slide view.
Reverse an action	From the Edit menu, choose Undo.
Save a new presentation	From the File menu, choose Save.
End a PowerPoint session	From the File menu, choose Exit.

For more information on	See the *Microsoft PowerPoint Handbook*
Understanding PowerPoint	Chapter 1, "Introducing PowerPoint"
Using PowerPoint	Chapter 3, "Working with PowerPoint Basics"

Preview of the Next Lesson

In the next lesson, you'll open an existing presentation and learn how take advantage of work that's already done by copying a slide and changing it slightly. You'll also learn how to rearrange slides in the Slide Sorter view, locate information in help, and enhance the look of your presentation. Finally, you'll print a presentation to include in your quick-reference notebook.

Working with an Existing Presentation

In order to work effectively in PowerPoint, you'll need to become familiar with all the features of the product. In the previous lesson, you learned how to enter title and body text, create new slides, change between Outline and Slide views, and move from slide to slide. In this lesson, you'll fill in the rest of the PowerPoint picture by learning how to open an existing presentation, incorporate slides from other presentations, rearrange slides in Slide Sorter view, change text styles, enter text in Notes view, locate information in Help, and print a presentation. The printed presentation will be the first few pages in your quick-reference notebook about PowerPoint. At the end of the lesson, your presentation will consist of the following slides:

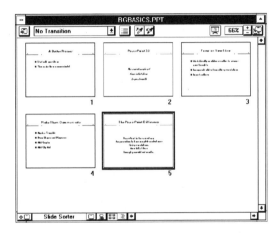

This lesson explains how to do the following:

- Open an existing presentation
- Incorporate slides from other presentations
- Rearrange slides
- Change text attributes
- Create speaker's note pages
- Locate information in Help
- Print a presentation

Estimated lesson time: 40 minutes

Opening a Presentation

If you haven't started PowerPoint yet, first work through "Getting Ready," beginning on page xiii.

As you learned in Lesson 1, a new, empty presentation window displays when you start PowerPoint. You can also open an existing presentation—one that you or a co-worker has already created—and work on it in the same way you would work on a new presentation. To open an existing presentation, you must first tell PowerPoint the name of the presentation and where it's located. You do this by using the Open command from the File menu.

Open a presentation

1   From the File menu, choose Open (CTRL+O) to display a list of presentations.

PowerPoint displays a dialog box in which you can select the name of the presentation you want. The dialog box you see might look different from the following, depending on where the practice files are located:

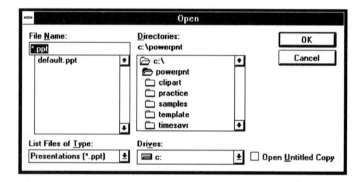

2   In the box under "Drives," check to be sure that drive C is selected (if that is where you stored your Step by Step practice files). Click the drop-down arrow next to the box to see and select from other listed drives.

If you do not see PRACTICE in the list of directories, see "Getting Ready," earlier in this book, for assistance.

3   In the list under "Directories," check to be sure that the PRACTICE directory is open. If it is not, select it by double-clicking it.

4   In the list of file names, select LESSON02.PPT.

A miniature picture of the first slide appears to the right as a preview of the presentation. If you can't remember the name of your presentation, you can select any of the available presentations for a preview.

Click here to get first slide miniature in Presentation Preview box

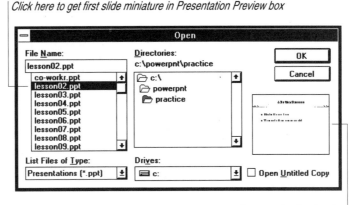

Presentation Preview box

5   Click the OK button.

PowerPoint closes the dialog box and displays the presentation LESSON02.PPT.

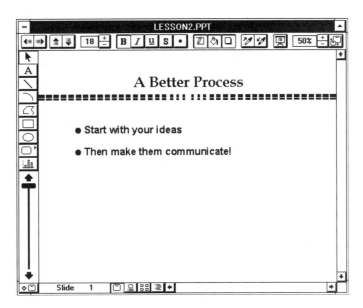

If you double-click the file name (LESSON02.PPT) from the Open dialog box, PowerPoint will open the file directly and you will not see the first slide in the Presentation Preview Box or need to click the OK button. When you open an existing presentation, PowerPoint closes the empty presentation window if you have not made any changes to it.

Save the presentation with a new name

In this lesson and the ones that follow, begin by giving the practice presentation a new name. When you rename a presentation, it's like making a copy of it to work on: Any changes you make do not affect the original. That way, if you want to go through a lesson again, the original practice file will be intact.

To choose a command, click the menu name near the top of the window, and then click the name of the command you want from the menu.

Italic indicates text that you supply; bold indicates text you should type exactly as it appears.

1 From the File menu, choose Save As.

PowerPoint displays the Save As dialog box in which you can type a new name for your presentation. The dialog box is the same one that appears when you save your presentation for the first time. For more information about using this dialog box, see "Saving the Presentation" in Lesson 1.

2 In the File Name box, type *your initials***basics**

Remember, this means that you type your initials with no space between them, followed by the word "basics." For example, if your initials are B. G., you would type **bgbasics.**

3 Click the OK button.

PowerPoint closes the dialog box and saves the presentation with the new name "BGBASICS.PPT," which displays in the Title bar above the Toolbar.

Note Presentations saved in Slide view will always open to the first slide no matter which slide displays when you save.

Preview the lesson

The presentation for this lesson contains reference information about working with an existing presentation. To preview the lesson, click the Slide Show button on the Toolbar and view the on-screen presentation.

Slide Show

1 On the Toolbar, click the Slide Show button.

PowerPoint displays the first slide in the presentation.

2 Click to advance to the next slide.

3 Click once for each slide to advance through the rest of the presentation.

After the last slide in the presentation, PowerPoint returns to the current view.

Incorporating Slides from Other Presentations

You can save time creating a presentation by using work that has already been done by a co-worker. Let's open a co-worker's presentation and copy slides from their presentation into your own. The incorporated slides conform to the characteristics of your presentation, so you don't have to make that many changes.

Change to Slide Sorter view

Slide Sorter View

▶ Click the Slide Sorter View button at the bottom of the window.

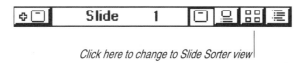

Click here to change to Slide Sorter view

All the slides appear in miniature on the screen, and the first slide is selected.

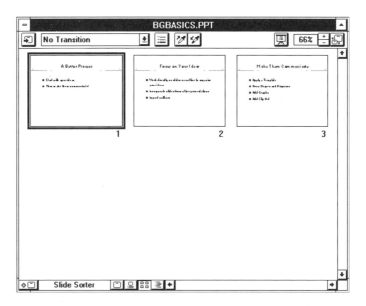

Open another presentation with slides

1 From the File Menu, choose Open.

PowerPoint displays the Open dialog box in which you can select the name of the presentation you want to open.

2 As you did at the beginning of this lesson, locate the PRACTICE subdirectory.

Refer to the beginning of this lesson for instructions, if necessary.

3   In the list of file names, select the CO-WORKR.PPT file.

4   Click the OK button.

The CO-WORKR.PPT presentation opens to the Slide Sorter view showing miniatures of the slides. The presentation opens in the view it was saved in prior to its last close.

Copy slides from one presentation to another in Slide Sorter view

1   From the Edit menu, choose Select All (CTRL+A).

A black rectangle appears around both slides indicating they are selected.

2   From the Edit menu, choose Copy (CTRL+C).

The slides are copied to the Windows Clipboard for temporary storage.

3   From the File menu, choose Close (CTRL+F4).

The presentation window closes and BGBASICS.PPT becomes active.

4   Click after the last slide in the presentation.

An insertion point appears after the slide. Since the slide is the last one in a row, the blinking insertion point appears in the next row. The slides copied from the other presentation will be inserted at this point. If you select a slide in the Slide Sorter view, then the slides copied from the other presentation appear after the selected slide.

5   From the Edit menu, choose Paste (CTRL+V).

The slides paste into your presentation. The pasted slides take on the characteristics of your presentation. PowerPoint makes it easy to incorporate slides from other presentations to efficiently create a new presentation.

6   Click in a blank area to the right of slide 5 to deselect the pasted slides.

When you paste slides in the Slide Sorter view, they remain selected until you deselect them.

Rearranging Slides in Slide Sorter View

After copying slides from the co-worker's presentation into your own, you'll want to rearrange the slides into the order that most effectively communicates your message. In Slide Sorter view you can drag slides from one location to another.

Move a slide in Slide Sorter view

▶   Click and drag slide 4, entitled "PowerPoint 3.0," to the left side of slide 2, entitled "Focus on Your Ideas."

You'll notice the pointer changes to a slide icon when you begin to drag. When you release the mouse, slide 4 moves to its new position as slide 2 and the other slides reposition.

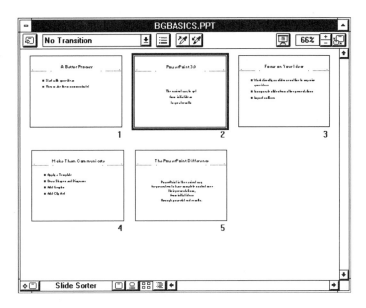

Change to Slide view

1   From the View menu, choose Slides.

PowerPoint changes to Slide view for slide 2.

Changing Text Attributes

Text can have attributes associated with it such as font type, size, and style as well as frame, fill, and shadow color. You can apply attributes to individual text or to an entire text object.

Change text attributes in Slide view

1   Click the lower text to select the Body object.

2   On the Toolbar, click the Italic button.

Italic

Click here for italic text

Font Size

3   On the Toolbar, click the Font size (+) button to increase the font size to 28 points.

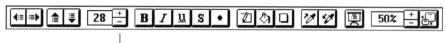

Click the + button or the - button to change font size

The font size increases in increments of more than one point at a time. For objects with different font sizes, clicking the font size buttons on the Toolbar increases or decreases font sizes in the selected object relative to their original settings.

4   From the Text menu, choose Font.

A submenu appears with more choices. Arial is the current font, which is indicated by a dot. Your list of fonts might be different than the ones shown.

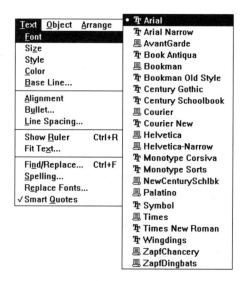

5   Select Times New Roman.

The Arial font changes to Times New Roman.

Your presentation window should look similar to the following illustration:

Entering Text in Notes View

In Notes view, you can create speaker's notes pages for your presentation. Each slide in your presentation has a corresponding note page. At the top of each note page is a reduced image of the accompanying slide for reference during the delivery of your presentation. To enter speaker's notes on a Note page, change to Notes view, select the Body object, and begin typing. Body text in Notes view works the same as it does in Slide view.

1 Click the up arrow on the Slide Changer to move to slide 1.

Slide Changer

2 Click the Notes View button at the bottom of the presentation window.

Notes View

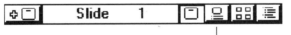

Click here to change to Notes view

Notes view appears at 33% view for most screens to display the entire screen. Your view scale might be different depending on the size of your monitor. At the top of the page, a reduced image of the slide displays, and at the bottom is a placeholder for body text.

Your presentation window should look similar to the following illustration:

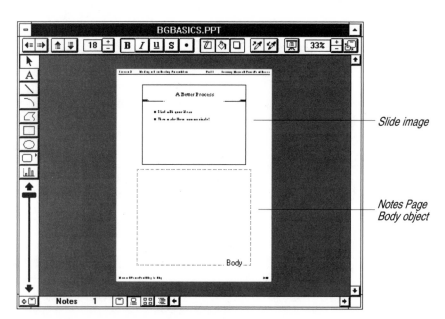

Slide image

Notes Page
Body object

3   Click the Notes Page Body object to select it.

View Scale

4   On the Toolbar, click the View Scale (+) button.

The view scale size increases from 33% to 50%, and displays the the selected Body object for the notes page.

5   Type the paragraph below without pressing the ENTER key. (If you make a mistake as you type, press the BACKSPACE key to delete the mistake, and type the correct text.)

If you are a presenter, you worry most about content when creating a presentation. PowerPoint makes it easy for you to get right to work entering your ideas, allowing you to decide how to make them communicate effectively later.

Move from note page to note page with the Slide Changer

In Notes view, the Slide Changer moves from note page to note page in the same way it does in Slide view.

1   Click the down arrow on the Slide Changer to view the other notes pages in the presentation until you reach notes page 5.

Slide View

2   Click the Slide View button.

Locating Information in Help

With PowerPoint Help you can quickly search the online Help topics for the specific information you need. Once a topic displays, you can select phrases that have solid underlines to jump to related topics. Within Help, you can view the contents list, search for a certain topic, move backward and forward through a Help topic, or display the history of Help topics you've viewed.

Search for a topic in Help

You've learned about Notes view. Now use Help for more information on Notes view.

1   Press the F1 key.

Pressing F1 displays the Help window. You can select any underlined topic and browse for information, or have PowerPoint search for what you need.

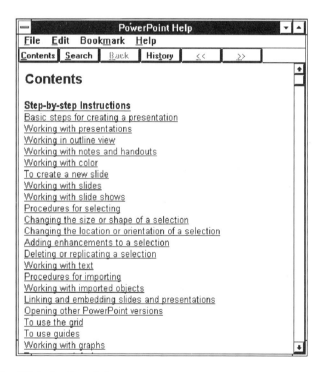

2   Click the Search button.

A search dialog box appears. You'll begin your search at the top of the dialog box by typing a word or selecting one from the list of categories. In the future, to go directly to this dialog box from PowerPoint, choose Search For Help On from the Help menu.

3 Type **notes** but do not press the ENTER key.

As you type, PowerPoint searches for categories of information associated with the word "notes." The categories are displayed in the middle box as shown below:

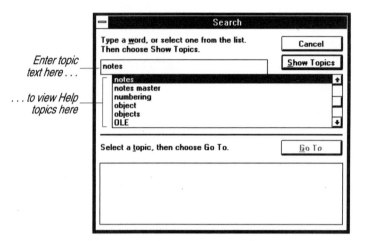

4 In the middle box, select the category "notes" if it's not already selected.

5 Click the Show Topics button.

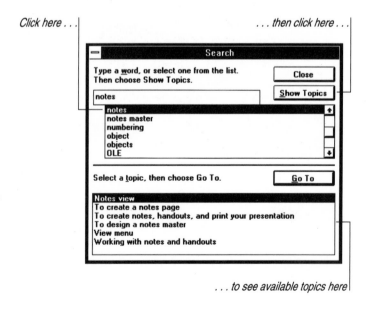

6 Select "To create a notes page" in the bottom box.

7 Click the Go To button.

PowerPoint displays information about creating a note page as well as other topics.

Jump to a related topic

If you do not see what you need in the selected Help topic, you can select any underlined phrase under "Related topics" to jump to related information.

1 Position your pointer over the underlined phrase "To design a notes master."

2 When the pointer changes to a hand, click.

Help jumps to information on designing a notes master. Take a moment to scroll through the topic, reading any definitions.

Return to the previous topic

You can backtrack through the Help topics that you've viewed.

1 Click the Back button.

PowerPoint displays the previous topic, "To create a notes page."

2 From the Help File menu, choose Exit to end your Help session.

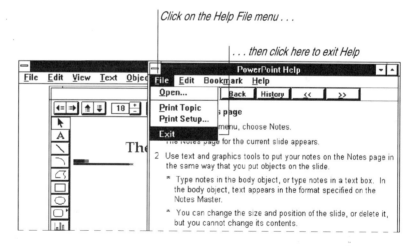

Ending your Help session closes the Help window and returns you to your presentation window.

TROUBLESHOOTING: **If you accidentally click the File menu on the presentation window**   Your PowerPoint presentation will become active. You'll need to make the Help window active again so you can exit Help. From the Help menu, choose Contents. From the PowerPoint Help File menu, choose Exit.

Printing a Presentation

PowerPoint is able to print your presentation in any of the four ways: Slides, Notes Pages, Handout (2, 3, or 6 per page), and Outline view to help you effectively present your message with the highest quality output.

If you are the only person who uses your computer and you have not yet printed a document using a Windows-based application, you might not yet have installed or selected a printer. If this is the case, take a moment and work through Appendix B, "Installing and Selecting a Printer." For complete instructions about installing and setting up a printer, see your Windows documentation. If you share this computer with others, it's likely that a printer is already installed and ready to use.

Print the quick-reference notebook presentation

For information on printing a presentation, refer to Lesson 13.

You can start your quick-reference notebook by printing your presentation.

1   From the File menu, choose Print (CTRL+P).

   The Print dialog box appears.

2   Click the down arrow next to the Print box.

3   Select Handouts (2 slides per page) from the drop-down list.

4   Click the OK button.

   A dialog box appears to give your printing status.

Save the presentation

▶   From the File menu, choose Save (CTRL+S).

   A dialog box doesn't appear because the presentation already has a name. The current information in your presentation is saved with the same name.

One Step Further

You have learned to open a presentation, change text attributes, copy and paste slides between presentations, rearrange slides in the Slide Sorter view, locate information in Help, and print a presentation. If you'd like to practice these and other basic skills in your practice presentation, try the following:

▶   While in Notes view, use the Text menu to change text styles and sizes.

▶   Move slides around in the Slide Sorter. Use the SHIFT key to select multiple slides.

▶   Enter text in the Body object. Use the outlining features you learned in Lesson 1.

▶   Search for topics of interest in Help.

If you want to continue to the next lesson

1 From the File menu, choose Close (CTRL+F4).

2 If a dialog box appears asking if you want to save the changes to your presentation, click the No button. You do not need to save the changes you made to the presentation after you printed it.

Choosing this command closes the active presentation; it does not exit PowerPoint. If no other presentations are open, the menu bar displays two available menus: File and Help.

If you want to quit PowerPoint for now

1 From the File menu, choose Exit.

2 If a dialog box appears asking if you want to save changes to the presentation, click the No button.

Lesson Summary

To	Do this
Open a presentation	Choose Open from the File menu. When the Open dialog box appears, select the file you want opened and click the OK button.
Copy slide(s) between presentations	Select slide(s) in the Slide Sorter or Outline views. From the Edit menu, choose Copy. Open another presentation where you want to paste the slides. Click the Slide Sorter View button and choose Paste from the File menu.
Rearrange slides in the Slide Sorter	Switch to Slide Sorter view. Click and drag slide to desired locations.
Change text to Bold, Italic, Underline, or Shadow	Select the text object or text and click the corresponding Toolbar button.
Change font size	Select the text object or text and click the (+) or (-) font size Toolbar buttons.
Enter text in Notes view	Click the Notes view button. Select the Body object and type.
Locate information in Help	Press F1. Select a topic name from the contents or click the Search button and type in a topic name.
Print a Presentation	From the File menu, choose Print. Select print options and click the OK button.

For more information on	See the *Microsoft PowerPoint Handbook*
Understanding PowerPoint	Chapter 1, "Introducing PowerPoint"
Using PowerPoint	Chapter 3, "Working with PowerPoint Basics"

Preview of the Next Lesson

In the next lesson, you'll import an existing outline, edit outline text and slides, and print an outline. You'll also learn how to rearrange text and slides in Outline view, and view your outline with only titles and unformatted text. By the end of the lesson, you'll have produced another presentation for your quick-reference notebook.

2 Organizing Your Ideas

Outlining Your Ideas

PowerPoint offers outlining abilities similar to Microsoft Word. Outline view shows you the slide title and body text for each slide in your presentation. The alternating sequence of titles and bodies forms an outline with each title appearing at the first level and the body appearing indented below. You can edit and rearrange both the title and body text in the Outline view. Your changes also appear in Slide view.

You can also import outlines created in other applications and print your outline. In this lesson, you'll create an outline, insert a Microsoft Word document, change the way you view your outline, rearrange text, change character attributes, and save an outline. At the end of the lesson, your presentation will consist of the following slides:

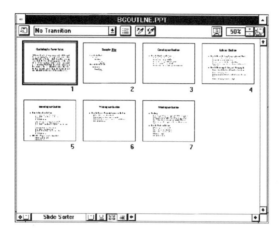

This lesson explains how to do the following:

- Work with an outline
- Insert an outline
- Change views of text in an outline
- Edit and rearrange outline text
- Format text and work with bullets
- Save an outline

Estimated lesson time: 40 minutes

Open a presentation

If you haven't already started PowerPoint, do so now. For instructions about starting PowerPoint, see "Getting Ready," earlier in this book.

1   From the File menu, choose Open (CTRL+O).

2   In the Directories box, be sure the PRACTICE directory is open. If it is not, select the drive where the Step by Step practice files are stored and open the appropriate directories to find the PRACTICE directory.

For information about opening a sample presentation, refer to Lesson 2.

3   In the list of file names, select LESSON03.PPT.

If you do not see LESSON03.PPT in the list of file names, check to be sure the correct drive and directory are selected. If you need help, see "Getting Ready."

4   Click the OK button.

Your presentation opens to the following slide:

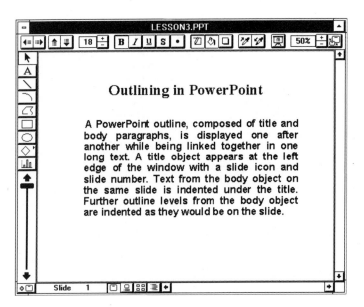

Save the presentation with a new name

Give the presentation a new name so the changes you make in this lesson will not overwrite the original presentation.

1   From the File menu, choose Save As.

2   In the File Name box, type *your initials***outlne**

For example, if your initials are B. G., type **bgoutlne**

3   Click the OK button.

Preview the lesson

The presentation for this lesson contains reference information about outlining your ideas. To preview the information in this lesson, click the Slide Show button on the Toolbar and view the on-screen presentation.

Slide Show

1 On the Toolbar, click the Slide Show button.

PowerPoint displays the first slide in the presentation.

2 Click to advance to the next slide.

3 Click once for each slide to advance through the rest of the presentation.

After the last slide in the presentation, PowerPoint returns to the current view.

Viewing Your Presentation in Outline View

In Outline view, each title appears on the left side of the window with a slide icon and slide number. Body text is indented under its title on the outline. If there are graphic objects on your slides, the slide icon appears with shapes inside.

Change to Outline view

Outline View

▶ Click the Outline View button.

A slide icon appears to the left of each slide title. Body text is indented one or more levels and the slide icon and title are selected.

Your presentation window should look similar to the following illustration:

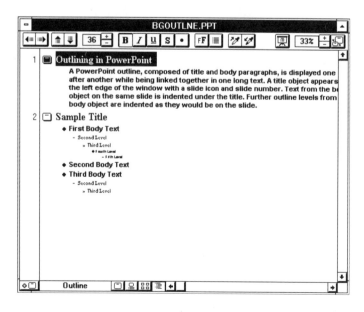

Inserting an Outline

PowerPoint inserts outlines created in other applications, such as Microsoft Word. When you insert a Microsoft Word document with outline heading styles, PowerPoint creates slide titles and bodies based on the heading and paragraph levels.

1   Position the I-beam cursor below the text of the last slide of the outline and click.

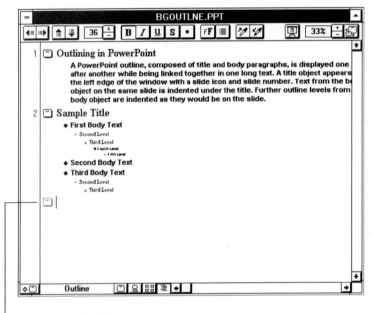

Gray slide icon placeholder

A gray slide icon appears. The gray slide icon is a placeholder for the next slide in the presentation. When you insert an outline or enter title or body text, PowerPoint creates new slides.

TROUBLESHOOTING: **If the gray slide icon doesn't appear**   Reposition the I-beam cursor below the text in the last slide and click.

2   From the Edit menu, choose Insert and then choose Outline.

3   In the Directories box, be sure the PRACTICE directory is open. If it is not, select the drive where the Step by Step practice files are stored and open the appropriate directories to find the PRACTICE directory.

4   Select OUTLINE.DOC from the list of file names.

If you do not see OUTLINE.DOC in the list of file names, check to be sure the correct drive and directory are selected. If you need help, see "Getting Ready."

5   Click the OK button.

A bar meter appears to show you the progress of reading the outline. After inserting an outline, the insertion point displays at the bottom of the outline.

Note   You can also open a Microsoft Word document to create a presentation using the Open command from the File menu and selecting Outlines from the List Files of Type.

Scrolling Through an Outline

The sample outline you're working on contains more text than you can see on the screen at one time. To see the rest of the text, you need to *scroll* through the outline. Scrolling means moving text across the screen to bring text that's currently above or below the window into view. You use the *scroll arrows* and the *scroll box* located on the *vertical* or *horizontal scroll bars* to move the outline through the window.

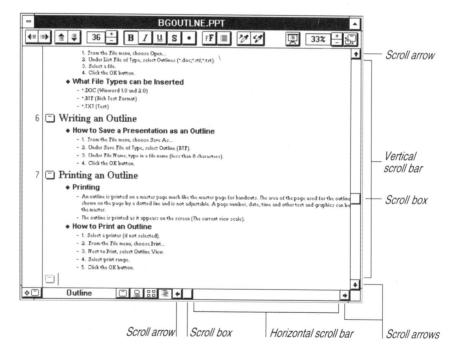

You can use any of three methods for scrolling, depending on how quickly you want to move through the outline. You can scroll line by line, window by window, or you can jump immediately to the beginning, middle, or end of the outline.

Scroll line by line

Each time you click a scroll arrow, PowerPoint changes the screen to show you
one more line.

1   Click the up scroll arrow a few times to see the text above the current
window display.

2   Click the down scroll arrow a few times to see the text below the window display.

3   Position your pointer over the down scroll arrow and hold the mouse button down.
To stop scrolling, release the mouse button.

The outline text "rolls" down the page. When you scroll to the end of the outline,
PowerPoint displays the blank space beyond the end of the text. The next
procedure shows you a fast way to get back to the top of the screen.

Jump to a different part of the outline

The following procedure shows you a quick way to jump to the beginning, middle, or
end of an outline, or anywhere in between.

1   Position your pointer over the scroll box and drag it to the top of the scroll bar—
you cannot drag it off the scroll bar—or press CTRL+HOME.

The beginning of the outline displays, as shown in the following illustration:

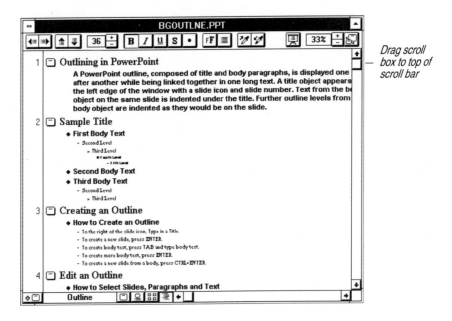

*Drag scroll
box to top of
scroll bar*

2   Drag the scroll box to the bottom of the scroll bar or press CTRL+END.

The end of the outline appears.

This method offers an advantage over scrolling line by line; the scroll box always stops at the last line of text or slightly below the last line. With this method you cannot scroll beyond the text you want to see.

Tip   You can drag the scroll box to any location on the scroll bar. For example, if you want to work on text that was in the middle of the outline, you can drag the scroll box halfway down the scroll bar.

Scroll window by window

Sometimes you need to move faster than line by line, but you don't need to scroll very far—the text you need to see is in the window area above or below the text currently displayed. The following procedure shows you the best shortcut for this situation.

1   Click above the scroll box in the scroll bar or press PAGE UP.

The window of text above what you are currently viewing appears.

2   Click below the scroll box or press PAGE DOWN.

The window of text below what you are currently viewing appears.

3   Scroll to the beginning of the outline. Position the I-beam cursor at the end of "Sample Title" in slide 2 and click.

Practice for a moment

You've learned three ways to scroll through an outline. If you frequently create outlines that are longer than one-half page, scrolling will be a skill you perform often.

- Click the up or down scroll arrow to scroll line by line.

- Practice dragging the scroll box to various positions on the scroll bar—first to the top, then to the middle, and then to the bottom.

- Click in the scroll bar above or below the scroll box to move one window at a time toward the beginning or end of the outline.

- When you've finished practicing, scroll to the beginning of the outline.

Viewing Your Outline

There are different ways of viewing your presentation in Outline view. You can collapse or expand your outline, use plain or formatted text, or change the view scale.

Titles Only

1   On the Toolbar, click the Titles Only button.

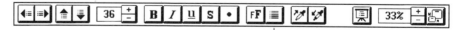

Click here to view only slide titles

The view switches from titles and bodies to titles only. The Titles Only button allows you to work with the main points of your outline.

Your presentation window should look similar to the following illustration:

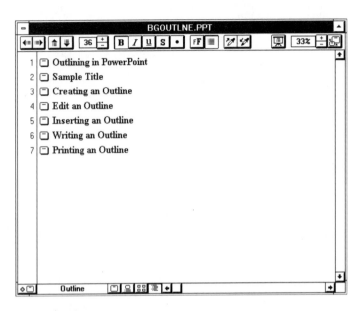

Titles Only

Draft Text

2   On the Toolbar, click the Titles Only button again.

The Outline view expands to include title and body text for the entire presentation.

3   On the Toolbar, click the Draft Text button.

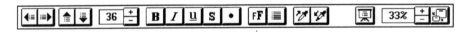

Click here to view with unformatted text

The view switches from formatted text to plain text as shown in the following illustration. The Draft Text button allows you to work with your content without formatting, so you can see your content easier. The formatting information remains, You can view it by clicking the Draft Text button again. When you print an outline, it will print with formatting on or off, depending on how you set the Draft Text button. Slide view will always include formatting when printing.

Your presentation window should look similar to the following illustration:

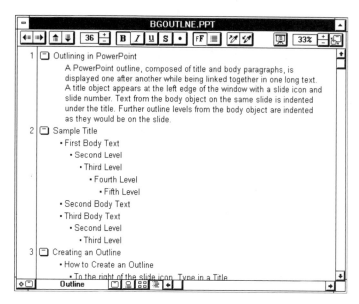

Draft Text

4 On the Toolbar, click the Draft Text button again.

The text in Outline view changes from unformatted to formatted text.

Editing and Rearranging in Outline View

In Outline view, you can edit and rearrange slides, paragraphs, and text by using the outline buttons on the Toolbar or by dragging.

Selecting Slides, Paragraphs, and Text

To edit and rearrange slides and paragraphs, you'll need to select the text first. To select a slide or paragraph, click the corresponding slide icon or body bullet to the left. To select text, position the I-beam cursor, click, and drag across the desired text block.

Select an entire slide

▶ Position the I-beam cursor (changes to four-headed arrow) over slide icon 1 and click to select the slide.

PowerPoint highlights the title and body text. The entire slide, including all text and graphic objects (even those that are not visible in Outline view), is selected. Also select a slide by clicking the slide number to the left of the slide icon.

Your presentation window should look similar to the following illustration:

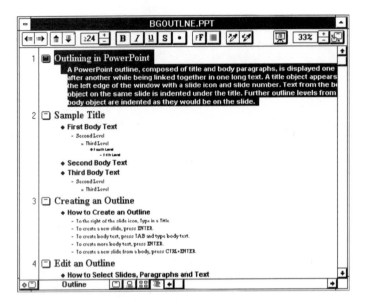

Note   Slide commands from the Edit menu (*Cut* or *Copy*) affect the entire slide, while text commands from the Text menu (*Font* or *Size*) affect only the Title and Body objects.

Select a paragraph

Selecting paragraphs works in the same way as selecting slides. A paragraph is text that begins and ends when you press the ENTER key.

▶ Position the I-beam cursor (changes to a four-headed arrow) over the bullet of the first paragraph entitled "First Body Text" in slide 2 and click.

PowerPoint selects the paragraph, including all related indented paragraphs, as shown in the following illustration:

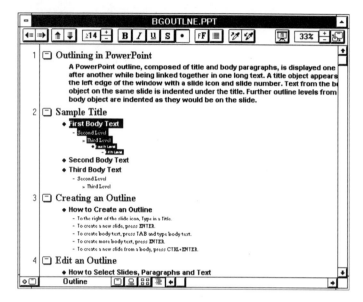

Select multiple paragraphs

1   Select the paragraph entitled "First Body Text" in slide 2.

2   Press and hold the SHIFT key and click the bullet for the paragraph entitled "Third Body Text." Notice that the second bullet point is also selected.

3   Press and hold the SHIFT key and click the bullet for the paragraph entitled "Second Body Text."

The paragraph entitled "Third Body Text" deselects.

Your presentation window should look similar to the following illustration:

Tip You can drag to select any amount of text. Click where you want the selection to begin, then while holding the SHIFT key, click where you want the selection to end. PowerPoint selects everything between the first click position and the last click position. You can also adjust any selection by holding down the SHIFT key and clicking where you want the selection to end.

Select text

Selecting text in Outline view is the same as selecting text in Slide view.

1 Position the I-beam cursor to the left of the word "Creating" in the title of slide 3.

2 Click and drag through the title "Creating an Outline" to select the title.

Rearranging Slides and Paragraphs

You can rearrange slides in Outline view by using the Move Up or Move Down buttons on the Toolbar or by dragging the slides and paragraphs to where you want them to appear.

Rearrange an entire slide

In Lesson 1, you learned how to move text in Outline view by using the Demote, Promote, Move Up, and Move Down buttons on the Toolbar. In this part of the lesson, you'll learn how to rearrange slides and text by dragging.

1 Position the four-headed arrow over the slide icon of slide 2 entitled "Sample Title," and then click and drag vertically to the top of the outline.

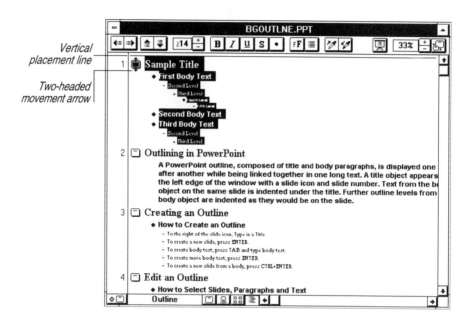

Vertical placement line

Two-headed movement arrow

2 Click and drag the slide icon entitled "Sample Title" back to its original position.

Tip   You can also choose the Undo command from the Edit menu to position the slide back to its original position.

Rearrange paragraphs

Paragraphs can be rearranged by dragging just as with slides.

1 In slide 2, position the four-headed arrow over the bullet to left of the text line entitled "Second Body Text."

2 Click and drag the text line horizontally to the right.

The text indents to the right. The paragraph is now a part of an indent level for "First Body Text."

Your presentation window should look similar to the following illustration:

Horizontal placement line

Two-headed movement arrow

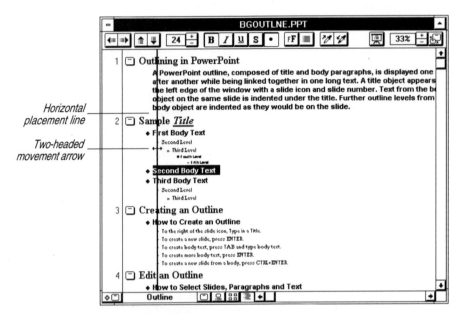

3   Click and drag the bullet entitled "Second Body Text" back to its original position.

Formatting Text

In Outline view, you can modify the style of the text by changing fonts, sizes, and styles just as you can in Slide view.

Format title and body text

1   Position the I-beam cursor to the right of the word "Title" in slide 2.

2   Click and drag left to select the word "Title."

3   On the Toolbar, click the Italic and Underline buttons.

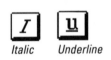

Italic   *Underline*

Click here for italic text | | Click here for underlined text

The selected text is now italicized and underlined.

4   In slide 2, position the I-beam cursor to the left of the word "First" in the first bullet point under the title.

If you move the cursor too far to the left, the cursor changes to the four-headed arrow.

5 Click and drag the I-beam cursor until it's positioned at the end of the bullet point entitled "Third Level."

The entire body text for slide 2 is selected as shown in the following illustration:

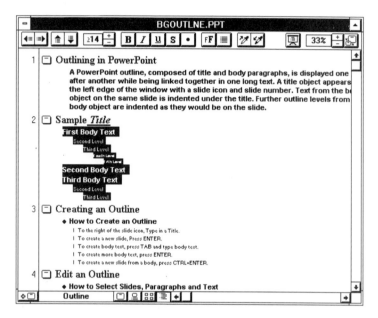

TROUBLESHOOTING: **If you drag past the end of the body or select too much text** Drag the I-beam cursor back up beyond the text you want to select. To ensure the selection of a specific text line when dragging, position the cursor over the text in that last line you want to select. If you select too much text, reposition the cursor to the left of the word "First," and then click and drag again.

Bullet

6 On the Toolbar, click the Bullet button.

Click here to turn bullets on or off

The bullets for the body turns off.

7 Click in the blank space to the right of slide 2.

The slide 2 body text deselects.

Saving an Outline

To save the outline for use in other applications, you must give the outline a name and store it on a disk. PowerPoint saves the outline in a format called *Rich Text Format* (RTF), which saves your text format. Other applications, like Word for Windows, can import your outlines saved in RTF.

Save as an outline

Use the following procedure to save the outline in the same directory with the Step by Step practice files. During the procedure, PowerPoint displays a *dialog box.* You use dialog boxes to give PowerPoint more information about what you want to do.

1   From the File menu, choose Save As.

PowerPoint displays the Save As dialog box. In the File Name box, BGOUTLNE, is selected.

2   Type your initials, with no periods or spaces, followed by the word **outrtf**

For example, if your initials are B. G., type **bgoutrtf**

Document names can be no more than eight characters long. They cannot have spaces in them.

3   In the Save File of Type box, click the drop-down arrow and select Outline (RTF).

4   In the Drives box, be sure that drive C is selected, if that is where you stored your Step by Step practice files. If you need assistance, see "Getting Ready," earlier in this book.

5   In the Directories box, be sure the PRACTICE directory is selected. If it is not, select it by double-clicking it.

6   Click the OK button.

The outline is saved as BGOUTRTF.RTF.

Note   The RTF outline, BGOUTRTF.RTF, is saved to the PRACTICE directory and does not appear on your screen as a presentation title.

Print the quick-reference notebook presentation in Outline view

1   From the File menu, choose Print.

The Print dialog box appears.

2   Click the down arrow next to the Print box.

3   Select Outline View from the drop-down list.

4   Click the OK button.

A dialog box appears to give your printing status.

Save the presentation in Outline view

PowerPoint saves your presentation in the current view and view scale. Choosing the Save command in Outline view saves your presentation in Outline view with the current view scale setting.

▶ From the File menu, choose Save.

When you open the presentation next time, PowerPoint will open in Outline view at the view scale it was last saved.

One Step Further

You have learned to insert an outline, change views of your outline, select and rearrange slides and paragraphs, save an outline in Rich Text Format, and print an outline. If you'd like to practice these and other basic skills in your practice presentation, try the following:

▶ Insert the outline you saved as *your initials***outrtf.rtf** into your presentation *initials***outlne.ppt**.

▶ Increase the view scale and scroll up and down using the three different methods you learned in this lesson.

▶ Select and move slides and paragraphs with Titles Only turned on by dragging or by using the Toolbar buttons.

▶ Select and change paragraph formats with the Titles Only option turned on by using the Toolbar buttons.

▶ Save your presentation as an outline in RTF.

▶ Print an outline with unformatted text using different view scales.

If you want to continue to the next lesson

1 From the File menu, choose Close (CTRL+F4).

2 If a dialog box appears asking if you want to save the changes to your presentation, click the No button. You do not need to save the changes you made to the presentation since you printed it.

Choosing this command closes the active presentation; it does not exit PowerPoint. If no other presentations are open, the menu bar displays two available menus: File and Help.

If you want to quit PowerPoint for now

1 From the File menu, choose Exit.

2 If a dialog box appears asking if you want to save changes to the presentation, click the No button.

Lesson Summary

To	Do this
Open a presentation	From the File menu, choose Open. When the Open dialog box appears, select the file you want opened and click the OK button.
View your slides in Outline view	Click the Outline view button.
Insert an outline	From the Edit menu, choose Insert Outline.
Scroll through an outline	Click scroll arrows, or click and drag the scroll box, or click above or below the scroll box.
View outline with Titles Only	On the Toolbar, click the Titles Only button.
View outline with Draft Text	On the Toolbar, click the Draft Text button.
Increase or decrease the Outline view size	On the Toolbar, click the View Scale buttons.
Switch Outline views	On the Toolbar, click the Home Scale button.
Select a slide or paragraph	Position the four-headed arrow to the left of the text and click.
Move a slide or paragraph	Select the slide or paragraph. On the Toolbar, click one of the Outlining buttons.
Save an outline	From the File menu, choose Save As and select File Type as Outline (RTF).
Print an outline	From the File menu, choose Print.

For more information on	See the *Microsoft PowerPoint Handbook*
Outlining in PowerPoint	Chapter 9, "Working with Outlines"
Printing in PowerPoint	Chapter 13, "Printing"

Preview of the Next Lesson

In the next lesson, you'll create text objects, change bullets, work with the ruler and tabs, change line spacing, and change text attributes. By the end of the lesson, you'll have produced another presentation for your quick-reference notebook.

Adding and Modifying Text

This lesson covers the basics of working with text in PowerPoint. Whether you're typing or editing text on a slide, outline, or speaker's notes page, you work with text the same way. In PowerPoint you can edit and outline your ideas throughout your entire presentation.

In this lesson, you'll learn how to create a text object, edit text, change the appearance of your text, check spelling, and find and replace text. At the end of the lesson, your presentation will consist of the following slides:

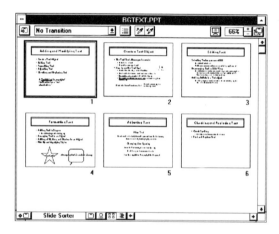

This lesson explains how to do the following:

- Add text to slides
- Edit and format text
- Align and arrange text
- Add bullets
- Change line spacing
- Check spelling
- Find and replace text

Estimated lesson time: 35 minutes

Open a presentation

If you haven't already started PowerPoint, do so now. For instructions about starting PowerPoint, see "Getting Ready," earlier in this book.

1 From the File menu, choose Open (CTRL+O).

2 In the Directories box, be sure the PRACTICE directory is open. If it is not, select the drive where the Step by Step practice files are stored and open the appropriate directories to find the PRACTICE directory.

For information about opening a sample presentation, refer to Lesson 2.

3 In the list of file names, select LESSON04.PPT.

If you do not see LESSON04.PPT in the list of file names, check to be sure the correct drive and directory are selected. If you need help, see "Getting Ready."

4 Click the OK button.

Your presentation opens to the following slide:

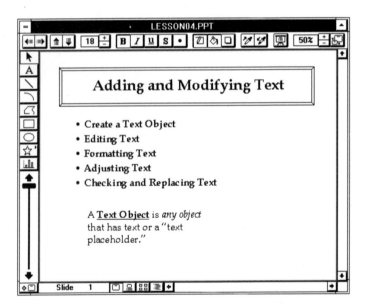

Save the presentation with a new name

Give the presentation a new name so the changes you make in this lesson will not overwrite the original presentation.

1 From the File menu, choose Save As.

2 In the File Name box, type *your initials***text**.

For example, if your initials are B. G., type **bgtext**

3 Click the OK button.

Preview the lesson

The presentation for this lesson contains reference information about PowerPoint text. To preview the information in this lesson, click the Slide Show button on the Toolbar and view the on-screen presentation.

Slide Show

1   On the Toolbar, click the Slide Show button.

PowerPoint displays the first slide in the presentation.

2   Click to advance to the next slide.

3   Click once for each slide to advance through the rest of the presentation.

After the last slide in the presentation, PowerPoint returns to the current view.

Change to the next slide

▶   Click the down arrow on the Slide Changer to advance to slide 2.

Adding Text

Usually, slides contain a Title object and a Body object. You can create other text on your slide or speaker's note page by using the Text tool. With the Text tool, you can create a text label—where text doesn't wrap—or a word processing box—where text wraps inside the boundaries of the box.

Creating a Text Object

A text object can be a text label or word processing box. To create a text label, click the Text Tool button from the Tool Palette, select a place for the text, click on the slide, and start typing. To create a word processing box, click and drag the text cursor on the slide and start typing.

Create a text label

A "text label" refers to text that is created without defining its boundaries by dragging a box, or text in which word-wrap has been turned off.

Text Tool

Text Cursor

1   On the Tool Palette, click the Text Tool button.

2   Position the cursor below the Body object on the slide.

The cursor changes from an arrow to the text cursor shown to the left.

3   Click once about an inch below the last line under the dash bullets.

A blinking insertion point appears. PowerPoint is ready for text.

4   Type **A text label doesn't word-wrap text**

Tip   A text label can be converted to a word processing box by changing it to word-wrap with the Fit Text command.

Your presentation window should look similar to the following illustration:

```
┌─────────────────────────────────────────────────────────┐
│ ─              BGTEXT.PPT                            ▲   │
├─────────────────────────────────────────────────────────┤
│ ◄═ ═►  ⬆ ⬇  18 ⊹  B I U S •  ▨ ◈ ▢  ✍ ✎  ▣  50% ⊹   │
│ ▶                                                        │
│ A    ┌──────────────────────────────────────────┐   ▲   │
│ ╲    │          Create a Text Object            │       │
│ ◿    │                                          │       │
│ ▢    │  • The Text Tool allows you to create:   │       │
│ ○    │       – A text label object              │       │
│ ☆ '  │       – A word-processing object         │  ┌──┐ │
│ ▥    │  • How to use the Text Tool              │  │A │ │
│      │       – On the Tool Palette, click the Text Tool └──┘ │
│ ⬆    │       – Position the text cursor in a blank area of the slide  Text Tool │
│ ▮    │       – To create a label object, click and start typing │
│ ▼    │       – To create a word-processing object, click and drag, then │
│      │         start typing                    │       │
│ ⬇    │                                          │       │
│      │     A text label doesn't word-wrap text│   ▼   │
│ ◇▢   │ Slide   2   ▢ ▯ ▦ ▤ ◄                    ►      │
└─────────────────────────────────────────────────────────┘
```

TROUBLESHOOTING: **If your text goes off the slide**   If your text accidently goes off the slide, PowerPoint adjusts the screen so you can continue to see your text. Press the BACKSPACE key to erase some text.

5   Move the cursor away from the text until it becomes the arrow cursor and click.

The text label deselects.

Create a word processing box

A"word processing box" refers to text that word-wraps within a defined box created by clicking and dragging.

Text Tool

┼

Cross Hair Cursor

1   On the Tool Palette, click the Text Tool button.

2   Position the cursor to the right of the text label on the slide.

3   Click and drag a box approximately two inches in length.

As you drag, the pointer changes to the cross hair cursor shown to the left. When you release the mouse button, a gray dotted rectangle appears. The gray dotted rectangle lets you know you're ready to edit the individual text box instead of an entire object.

4   Type **A word processing box word-wraps text**

Tip   A word processing box can be converted to a text label by turning off the word-wrap option. Use the Fit Text command to change the word-wrap option.

Your presentation window should look similar to the following illustration:

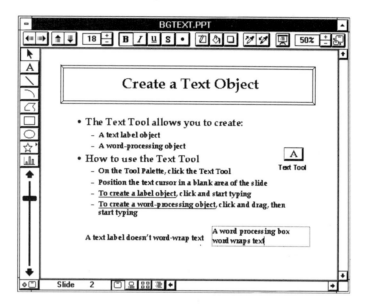

5   Click outside the gray rectangle to deselect the text box.

Note   Text created with the Text tool isn't entered in the Title or Body objects and doesn't appear in Outline view. Only the title and body text appear in Outline view. Text that appears in Slide view but is not a part of the Title object or Body object can be edited only in Slide view. Title text and body text can be edited in either Slide view or Outline view.

Change to the next slide

▶   Click the down arrow on the Slide Changer to advance to slide 3.

Editing Text

You might find you'll need to edit text while in Slide view. Editing text in Slide view is similar to editing text in Outline view.

Select text to edit

1   Click the body text to select the Body object.

2 Position the pointer to the right of the word "click" in the line "Put the arrow cursor where..." and click to position the insertion point.

Your presentation window should look similar to the following illustration:

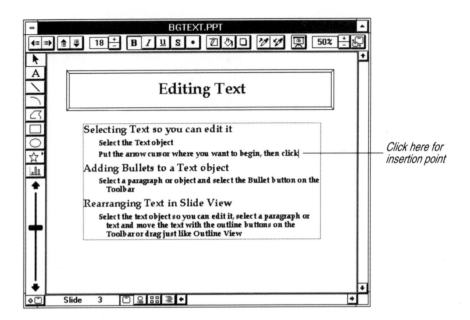

Click here for insertion point

A dotted rectangle appears around the text object, and a blinking insertion point appears where you clicked. The dotted rectangle means you can work with individual text.

3 Press the SPACEBAR and type **and start typing**

The text word-wraps to the next line. The size of the Body object adjusts to contain the new text. (With the I-beam cursor, you can place the insertion point in another position and select text to edit or rearrange.)

Rearrange text in Slide view

1 Position the I-beam cursor to the left of the text line entitled "Adding Bullets to a Text object" until the I-beam cursor changes to the four-headed arrow.

2 Click and drag the selected text to the bottom of the text object.

The second bullet point moves into the third position. Rearranging text in Slide view works in the same manner as it does in Outline view.

Your presentation window should look similar to the following illustration:

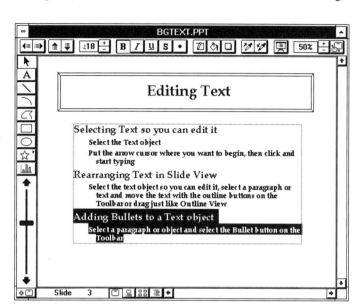

When a gray dotted line surrounds a text object, PowerPoint can edit individual text, permit a word or text range to be selected, or allow additional text to be entered. A selection box (fuzzy box) around an object indicates you're ready to edit the entire object.

Add bullets

1   From the Edit menu, choose Edit Object (CTRL+E).

The edit changes from individual text to the entire object.

Bullet

2   On the Toolbar, click the Bullet button.

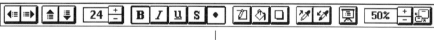

Click here to turn bullets on or off

The bullets turn on at every level of the text. The Bullet button works the same in Slide view as it does it Outline view.

Change to the next slide

▶   Click the down arrow on the Slide Changer to advance to slide 4.

Formatting Text

Text attributes, such as italic, bold, underline, shadow, and size can be changed with commands from the Text menu. To apply attributes to title or body text, use the text attribute buttons on the Toolbar.

Add text to a shape

You can add text to a shape by selecting the shape and typing.

1 Click the star object to select it.

2 Type **Great!**

3 Position the pointer over the border of the voice bubble object and click.

Note You must click the border (or the text) of an object that has no fill to select the object.

---

4 Type **Arranging text in a shape is easy**

Text in the bubble object extends beyond the edges of the shape because the word-wrap option is initially turned off, as shown in the following illustration:

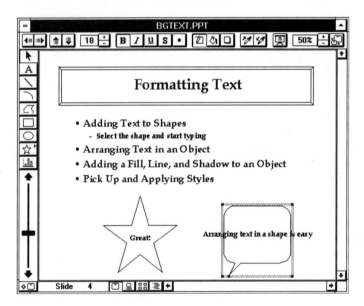

Format text in a shape

1 Select the voice bubble object by clicking its border.

2 On the Toolbar, click the Italic button.

The text in the object changes to Italic.

3 On the Toolbar, click the Font Size button (+) twice.

The font size changes to 24 points.

4 On the Toolbar, click the Fill button.

Italic

Font size

Fill

Click here to turn object fill on

The text object is filled with the color scheme fill color.

Note The default color for object fill in a new presentation is white. For the presentation you are working on, the default fill color has been changed to gray to match the color scheme menu.

S

Text Shadow

5 On the Toolbar, click the Text Shadow button.

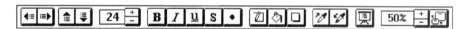

Click here to turn text shadow on

The text in your voice bubble is now shadowed.

Your presentation window should look similar to the following illustration:

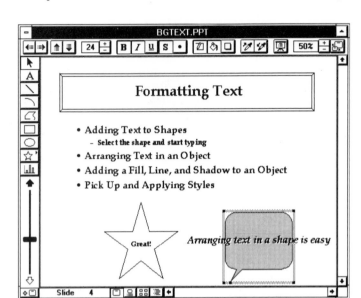

Format text with Pick Up Style and Apply Style commands

Using the Pick Up Style and Apply Style commands, you can pick up a set of styles from selected text and objects and apply them to other selected text and objects.

1   On the Toolbar, click the Pick Up Style button.

Pick Up Style

Click here to pick up text and object attributes

PowerPoint picks up and stores the specific text and object styles of the selected object and text.

2   Click inside star object to select it.

Note   Since the star object is filled with white, clicking within the borders of the star will select it. This is an easy way to determine if an object has a fill.

Apply Style

3   On the Toolbar, click the Apply Style button.

Click here to apply text and object attributes

PowerPoint changes the text style and fill color of the star object by applying the style you picked up from the voice bubble object.

TROUBLESHOOTING: **If the star object does not look like the voice bubble**   The Pick Up tool works only when you select an object. You may have clicked the Pick Up tool while no object was selected, or while a different object was selected. Repeat steps one through three after selecting the voice bubble object.

Your presentation window should look similar to the following illustration:

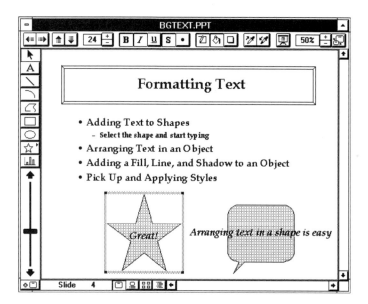

Change to the next slide

▶   Click the down arrow on the Slide Changer to advance to slide 5.

Adjusting Text

You have complete control over the placement and position of your text in PowerPoint. You can adjust the alignment, line spacing, and arrangement of text in an object to achieve the best look.

Turn bullets off

1   Click the body text to select it.

2   On the Toolbar, click the Bullet button.

The bullets turn off at every level of text.

Bullet

Change text alignment

▶   From the Text menu, choose Alignment and then choose Center (CTRL+\).

The text alignment in the body object moves to the center.

Change line spacing

1   From the Text menu, choose Line Spacing.

The Line Spacing dialog box appears, showing the current spacing settings for lines and paragraphs.

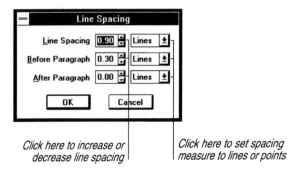

Click here to increase or decrease line spacing   *Click here to set spacing measure to lines or points*

2   Click the Up Arrow in the Line Spacing box until the line spacing is set to 1.20.

Notice that the text on the slide changes each time you click the line spacing buttons in the dialog box. If you hold down the mouse when you click the Up or Down Arrow buttons, the number will continue to change.

3   Click the OK button.

Arrange text in an object

1   Click inside the cross object to select it.

2   From the Text menu, choose Fit Text.

The Fit Text dialog box appears. If you can't see the cross object because the Fit Text dialog box is covering it, click the dialog box Title bar and drag it until you can completely see the cross object.

3   Click the Word-wrap Text in Object check box.

Word-wrap turns off and the text adjusts to no longer wrap to the object.

4 Click the Adjust Object Size to Fit Text check box.

Adjust Object Size turns on and the object changes to adjust to the text.

5 Click the Adjust Object Size to Fit Text check box again.

Adjust Object Size turns on.

6 In the Anchor Point box, click the drop-down arrow and select Middle.

The text in the object moves to the middle of the shape. The Fit Text dialog box should look similar to the following illustration:

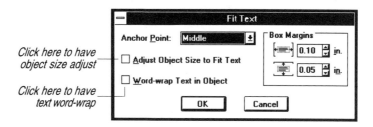

7 Click the OK button.

Change to the next slide

▶ Click the down arrow on the Slide Changer to advance to slide 6.

Checking and Replacing Text

The spelling checker checks the spelling of the entire presentation, including all slides, outlines, note pages, handout pages, and all four master views. PowerPoint uses a built-in dictionary to check your presentation. If the PowerPoint dictionary finds a word it doesn't recognize, you can add the word to the PowerPoint custom dictionary. You can also use custom dictionaries from other Microsoft applications.

Checking Spelling

1 From the Text menu, choose Spelling.

2   Click the Check Spelling button.

PowerPoint begins checking the spelling on the current slide.

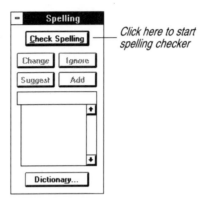

Click here to start
spelling checker

3   The spelling checker stops and selects the misspelled word "Dictionry."

4   Click the Suggest button.

A list appears in the middle box showing possible correct spellings of the
misspelled word "Dictionry."

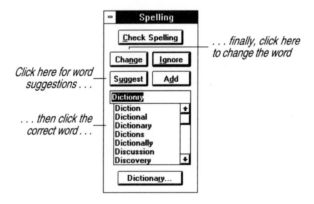

Click here for word
suggestions . . .

. . . then click the
correct word . . .

. . . finally, click here
to change the word

5   Select the word "Dictionary" from the list of suggested words.

6   Click the Change button to correct the spelling.

Use the custom dictionary

The custom dictionary allows you to add words that the PowerPoint dictionary doesn't
recognize. Click the Dictionary button in the Spelling dialog box to add a word to your
custom dictionary. You can also delete words you've added to your custom dictionary.

1   Click the Check Spelling button again.

The spelling checker stops when it fails to recognize the word "PowerPoint" on the Notes Master.

2 Click the Dictionary button.

The Custom Dictionary dialog box appears.

3 Click the (+) button.

The custom dictionary adds the word "PowerPoint."

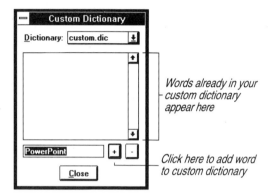

4 Click the Close button.

Continue spelling and change words

1 Click the Check Spelling button.

A dialog box appears indicating the spelling checker has reached the end of the presentation.

2 Click the Continue button to finish checking your presentation.

The spelling checker stops at the word "Toolbar."

3 Click the Add button.

The word "Toolbar" is added to your custom dictionary. A dialog box appears when the spelling checker has completed looking for misspelled words.

4 Click the OK button.

5 From the File menu, choose Close (CTRL+F4).

The Spelling dialog box closes.

Replacing Text

1 From the Text menu, choose Find/Replace (CTRL+F).

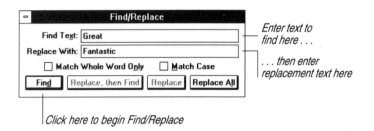

Enter text to find here . . .

. . . then enter replacement text here

Click here to begin Find/Replace

2 In the Find Text box, type **Great**

3 Press TAB or click the I-beam cursor in the Replace With box.

4 Type **Fantastic**

5 Click the Find button.

PowerPoint finds the word "Great" on slide 4. Click and drag the Title bar to see the selected text.

6 Click the Replace button.

7 Click the Find button.

A dialog box appears indicating the Find/Replace has reached the end of the presentation.

8 Click the Cancel button.

9 Double-click the Find/Replace Control-menu box.

Double-click here to close dialog box

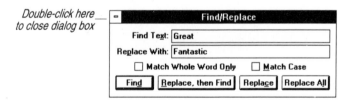

The Find/Replace dialog box closes.

Print the quick-reference notebook presentation

For information on printing a presentation, refer to Lesson 13.

1 From the File menu, choose Print (CTRL+P).

The Print dialog box appears.

2 Click the down arrow next to the Print box.

3   Select Handouts (2 slides per page) from the drop-down list.

4   Click the OK button.

A dialog box appears to give your printing status.

Save the presentation

▶   From the File menu, choose Save (CTRL+S).

A dialog box doesn't appear because the presentation already has a name. The current information in your presentation is saved with the same name.

One Step Further

You have learned to create and edit a text object, format text using the Toolbar, adjust text alignment and line spacing, check spelling, and find and replace text. If you'd like to practice these and other basic skills in your practice presentation, try the following:

▶   Create text labels and word processing boxes. Convert a text label to a word processing box and vice versa. (Hint: Use the Fit Text command.)

▶   Select a text object and rearrange its text using the Outline buttons on the Toolbar and by dragging.

▶   Create text objects and use the Fill command to change the fill.

▶   Select a text object, adjust the Fit Text margins, and change the word-wrap settings.

▶   Select a text object and adjust the Before and After Paragraph line spacing.

If you want to continue to the next lesson

1   From the File menu, choose Close (CTRL+F4).

2   If a dialog box appears asking if you want to save the changes to your presentation, click the No button. You do not need to save the changes you made to the presentation since you printed it.

Choosing this command closes the active presentation; it does not exit PowerPoint. If no other presentations are open, the menu bar displays two available menus: File and Help.

If you want to quit PowerPoint for now

1   From the File menu, choose Exit.

2   If a dialog box appears asking if you want to save changes to the presentation, click the No button.

Lesson Summary

To	Do this
Create a text label object	Click the Text Tool button. Click on the slide and type.
Create a text word processing box	Click the Text Tool button. Click and drag on the slide to create a text box, and then type.
Select text to edit	Select the text object, and click the text to place the insertion point.
Rearrange text in Slide view	Select text. Click and drag paragraphs.
Add text to a shape	Select the shape and type.
Arrange text in an object	Select an object with text. From the Edit menu, choose Fit Text.
Format text in a shape	Select the shape and choose styles from the Toolbar or Text menu.
Format text with Pick Up and Apply Styles	Select an object. On the Toolbar, click Pick Up Style. Select another object. On the Toolbar, click Apply Style.
Change text alignment	Select a text object. From the Text menu, choose Alignment.
Change line spacing	Select a text object. From the Text menu, choose Line Spacing.
Check Spelling	From the Text menu, choose Spelling.
Find and Replace text	From the Text menu, choose Find/Replace.

For more information on	See the *Microsoft PowerPoint Handbook*
Text in PowerPoint	Chapter 7, "Working with Text"
Advanced text features	Chapter 8, "Using Special Text Features"

Preview of the Next Lesson

In the next lesson, you'll change the Slide Master, change bullets, work with the ruler and tabs, apply a template, and change PowerPoint defaults. By the end of the lesson, you'll have produced another presentation for your quick-reference notebook.

3 Making Your Ideas Communicate

Changing Masters and Applying Templates

PowerPoint uses Masters to help create professional looking slides, audience handouts, and speaker's note pages. A Master is a set of formatting characteristics, graphics and text placement that is consistent throughout the entire presentation. Items from a Master can be set individually to apply to any or all slides, handout pages, or speaker's note pages. A template is a presentation that has a set of color and text characteristics that can be "applied" to your presentation. PowerPoint comes with over 160 templates that are professionally designed to work well in different output formats: black and white, color overhead, on-screen, or color overheads.

In this lesson, you'll learn how to format the Master Title and Master Body, add background objects to masters, add page number object to a master, change the default font setting, and apply a PowerPoint template. At the end of the lesson, your presentation will consist of the following slides:

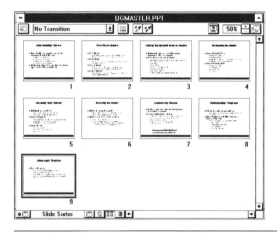

This lesson explains how to do the following:

- Understand and view a master
- Add background items to a master
- Format a Master Title and Body
- Adjust body indents
- Customize the default settings
- Apply a template

Estimated lesson time: 25 minutes

Open a presentation

If you haven't already started PowerPoint, do so now. For instructions about starting PowerPoint, see "Getting Ready," earlier in this book.

1 From the File menu, choose Open (CTRL+O).

2 In the Directories box, be sure the PRACTICE directory is open. If it is not, select the drive where the Step by Step practice files are stored and open the appropriate directories to find the PRACTICE directory.

For information about opening a sample presentation, refer to Lesson 2.

3 In the list of file names, click LESSON05.PPT.

If you do not see LESSON05.PPT in the list of file names, check to be sure the correct drive and directory are selected. If you need help, see "Getting Ready."

4 Click the OK button.

Your presentation opens to the following slide:

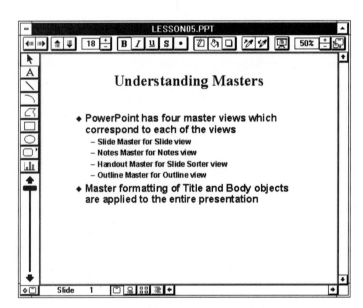

Save the presentation with a new name

Give the presentation a new name so the changes you make in this lesson will not overwrite the original presentation.

1 From the File menu, choose Save As.

2 In the File Name box, type *your initials***master**

For example, if your initials are B. G., type **bgmaster**

3 Click the OK button.

Preview the lesson

The presentation for this lesson contains reference information about PowerPoint
Masters and Templates. To preview the information in this lesson, click the Slide
Show button on the Toolbar and view the on-screen presentation.

Slide Show

1   On the Toolbar, click the Slide Show button.

PowerPoint displays the first slide in the presentation.

2   Click to advance to the next slide.

3   Click once for each slide to advance through the rest of the presentation.

After the last slide in the presentation, PowerPoint returns to the current view.

Understanding PowerPoint Masters

Each PowerPoint view has a corresponding Master—Slide Master for Slide view,
Notes Master for Notes view, Handout Master for Slide Sorter view, and Outline
Master for Outline view. When you add an object or change text format on a master,
the corresponding changes are made in that view. The Slide Master, for example,
controls the format of the Title and Body objects for each slide in your presentation.
Adding graphics and text to a Slide Master places them on every slide.

View the Slide Master

1   From the View menu, choose Slide Master.

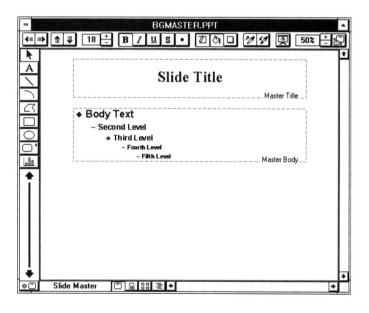

The Slide Master contains a Master Title and a Master Body. The Master Title and Body control the text format for your slide presentation. For example, when you change the text format to italic in the Master Title, the title on each slide changes to to italic to follow the master. In PowerPoint, you're always in control; if you don't want to follow the Slide Master for any reason, you have the choice to turn it off.

2 From the View menu, choose Slides.

PowerPoint returns you to the first slide.

Change to the next slide

1 Click the down arrow on the Slide Changer to advance to slide 2.

Read about the PowerPoint Masters.

Slide Changer

2 Click the down arrow on the Slide Changer to advance to slide 3.

Adding Background Items to Masters

You can add background items such as shapes, text headings, the date and time, page numbers, pictures, and graphics to all of the master views. The Master background items appear on the corresponding views.

Add a text label to the Slide Master

Slide View

1 Click the depressed Slide View button.

Note Clicking a depressed view button takes you to the master for that view.

Text Tool

2 On the Tool Palette, click the Text Tool button.

3 Position the text cursor in a blank area below the Master Body.

4 Click and type **PowerPoint 3.0**

5 Click in a blank area of the master to deselect the text object.

6 Click and drag the text object to the lower left corner of the Slide Master.

Your presentation window should look similar to the following illustration:

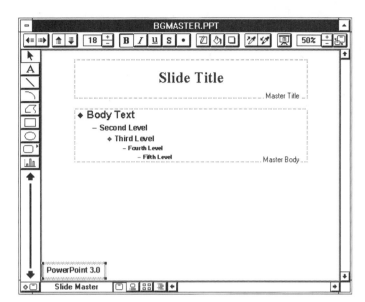

Add a page number

1   Click in a blank area to deselect the text object.

2   From the Edit menu, choose Insert, and then choose Page Number.

A small text object displaying two pound symbols appears in the middle of your screen.

Note   If a text object is selected when you insert the page number, the page number will be positioned at the end of the text in that object.

PowerPoint replaces this symbol with the date when your presentation is printed or displayed in a slide show. You can also add the time or date to your presentation by choosing the Insert Time or Page Number command from the Text menu. The date, page numbers, and time do not show up on individual slides, but do appear on the printed slide.

3   Click and drag the Page Number object to the upper right side of your slide.

Your presentation window should look similar to the following illustration:

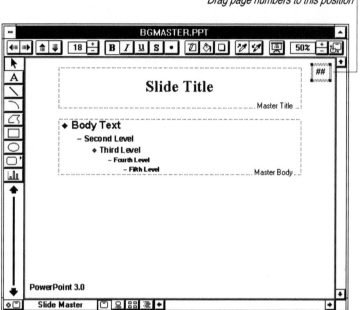

Add a header to the Outline Master

1   From the View menu, choose Outline Master.

The Outline Master appears with a placeholder (dotted rectangle) in the middle of the presentation window. The placeholder lets you know where your outline text is placed on the Outline Master when printing. You can add background items outside the Outline placeholder without interfering with the outline text.

Text Tool

2   On the Tool Palette, click the Text Tool button.

3   Place your text cursor just above the left corner of the Outline placeholder and click.

4   Type **PowerPoint 3.0 Master and Template Outline**

Your presentation window should look similar to the following illustration:

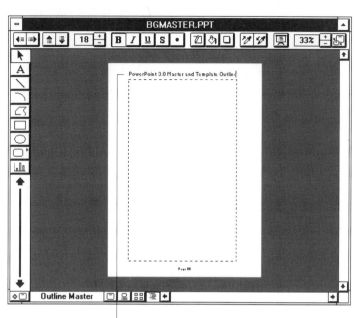

Position pointer here and click to add text

Note Both the Outline Master and Handout Master display placeholders (dotted lines) that indicate the text borders for those views. **Do not** place background items over the placeholder lines because the background items will interfere with the printed outline or handout.

Slide View

5 Click the Slide View button twice.

PowerPoint switches to the Slide Master.

Formatting the Master Title and Body

Every PowerPoint presentation has a Slide Master that contains a Master Title object and a Master Body object. Formatting these objects in the Master view provides consistency for your presentation. The Master Title object and Body object determine the style and placement of your slides' Title and Body objects.

1 Click anywhere in the Master Title object.

The text object is selected showing the current font size as 36 point, as displayed on the Toolbar.

Font Size

Italic

2 On the Toolbar, click the Font Size (+) button to increase the font size to 40 point.

3 Click the Master Body object to select it.

4 Click to the right of the word "Text."

The blinking insertion pointer is placed next to the word "Text."

5 Click to the right of the word "Text" and drag left to select the line.

6 From the Text menu, choose Font, and then choose Courier New.

7 On the Toolbar, click the Italic button.

8 Click outside the Master Body object in a blank area to deselect it.

Your Slide Master should look similar to the following illustration:

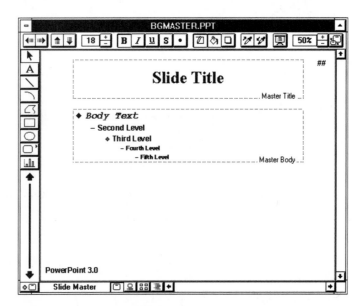

9 From the View menu, choose Slides.

The body text at the first level changes to Courier New throughout the presentation.

Your presentation window should look similar to the following illustration:

```
┌─────────────────────────────────────────────────┐
│ ▭              BGMASTER.PPT                    ▲ │
├─────────────────────────────────────────────────┤
│ ⟵ ⟶ | ⇞ ⇟ | 18 ± | B  I  U  S  • | ▨ ▨ ▯ | ▨ ▨ | ▨ | 50% ± ▨ │
├─────────────────────────────────────────────────┤
│ ▶                                             ▲ │
│ A      Adding Background Items to      ##       │
│ ╲              Masters                          │
│ ◠                                               │
│ ◿      ◆ Background items you put on the        │
│ ▭        masters appear on all the slides or    │
│ ○        pages                                  │
│ ▭      ◆ Add a Background item to masters       │
│ ▥        – In Slide View, click the Slide View button to go to the │
│ ⬆          Slide Master (This works for all masters) │
│            – Draw shapes                        │
│ ▬          – Add text objects                   │
│            – Add date, time, or page number     │
│            – Add pictures or graphics           │
│            – Choose a color scheme              │
│            – Click the View button to go back to Slide View │
│ ⬇   PowerPoint 3.0                              │
├─────────────────────────────────────────────────┤
│ ⬦▭    Slide   3   ▯ ▯ ▦ ▤ ◆              ▶ │
└─────────────────────────────────────────────────┘
```

Change to the next slide

▶ Click the down arrow on the Slide Changer to advance to slide 4.

Notice the background items and font changes you made to the Slide Master appear on this slide.

Format bullets

PowerPoint allows you to customize the bullets in your presentation for individual paragraphs or entire objects.

Slide View

1 Click the depressed Slide View button.

The Slide Master appears.

2 Click the Master Body object to select it.

3 Position the pointer anywhere on the first line of text entitled "Body Text" in the Master Body object.

4 Click to place the insertion point on the line.

5 From the Text menu, chose Bullet.

The Bullet dialog box appears with the Monotype Sorts symbol font. The current bullet symbol is selected. You can change the symbol font in the Bullets From drop-down list, adjust the percentage of the font size, or choose a special color.

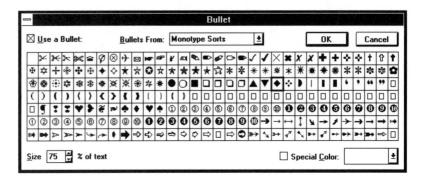

6 Select a bullet item from the dialog box.

7 Click the OK button.

The bullet you selected is placed in the first line of text.

8 From the View menu, choose Slides.

PowerPoint returns to slide 4 and shows the bullet change.

Change to the next slide

▶ Click the down arrow on the Slide Changer to advance to slide 5.

Adjusting Body Indents

PowerPoint uses indents to control the distance and location between bullets and text levels. To work with indented text and bullets, select a text object and show its ruler to make adjustments. Adjusting indents in PowerPoint works the same way as it does in Microsoft Word for Windows.

Displaying the Ruler

Slide View

1 Click the depressed Slide View button.

The Slide Master appears.

2 Click the Master Body object to select it.

3 From the Text menu, choose Show Ruler (CTRL+R).

Your presentation window should look similar to the following illustration:

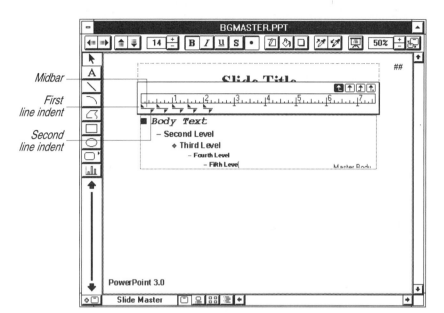

Set Indent Markers

The indent markers on the ruler control the five indent levels of the Body object. Each indent level consists of two indent markers (or triangles) separated by a horizontal line, called a *midbar*. The upper triangle controls only the first line of the paragraph; the bottom triangle controls the left edge of the paragraph text. Each indent level is set so the first line extends to the left of the paragraph, with the rest of the paragraph "hanging" below it. This indent setting is called a *hanging indent*.

Adjust indent markers

1   Move your pointer over the bottom triangle of the first indent level.

2   Click and drag the bottom triangle to the left margin of the ruler.

When you release the mouse button, the text for level one moves next to the bullet point on the left margin.

Your ruler and Master body should look similar to the following illustration:

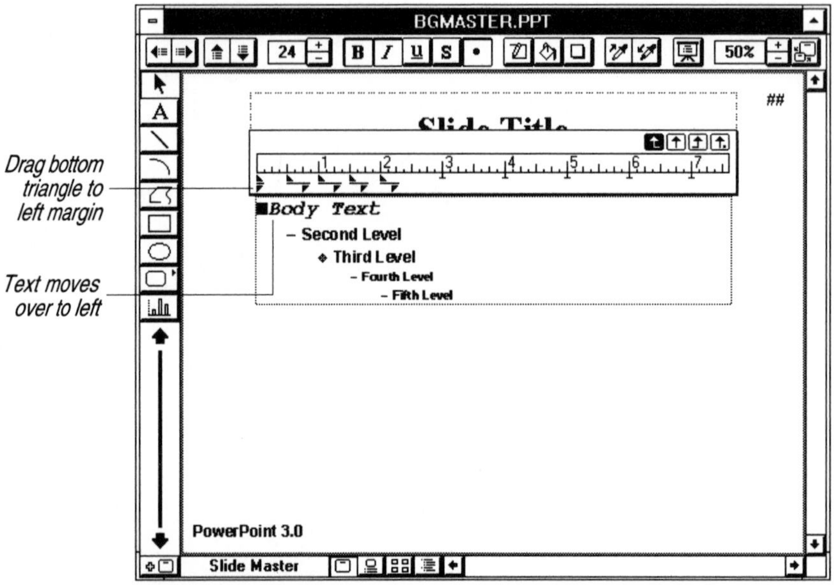

Drag bottom triangle to left margin

Text moves over to left

Adjust the margin level

1 Click and slowly drag the midbar of the first indent level to the 0.5 inch mark on the ruler.

Note If you drag an indent level or marker into another indent level, the first indent level (or marker) will push the second indent level until you release the mouse button. To move an indent marker back to its original position, click and drag the indent level's midbar.

Your presentation should look similar to the following illustration:

Moving the first indent marker repositions the left margin of the Body object to the 0.5 inch mark. (Notice the first text level in the Body object.)

TROUBLESHOOTING: **If your ruler looks different**   If the ruler on your screen looks different from the one in the above illustration, you might not have moved the indent marker's midbar. If the indent markers are not aligned over one another, click and drag one of the markers back to the other.

2   Drag the upper triangle of the first indent marker to the left edge of the ruler.

Drag the upper triangle of the first indent marker to the left edge of the ruler.

The first indent level of your ruler is formatted again as a hanging indent.

Your presentation window should similar to the following illustration:

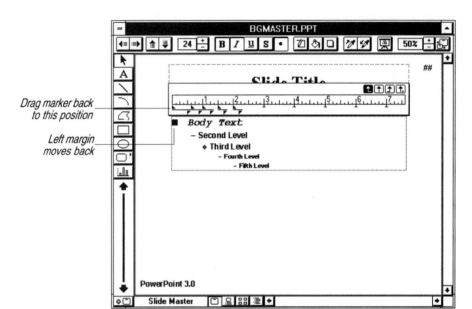

3 From the Text menu, choose Hide Ruler.

4 From the View menu, choose Slides.

PowerPoint returns you to slide 5.

Change to the next slide

▶ Click the down arrow on the Slide Changer to advance to slide 6.

Following the Master

In PowerPoint you have control of the Master views. Each slide can be individually set to follow the Master view by selecting certain options from the Follow Master command. The Follow Master command controls the presentation color scheme, background items, and the Title and Body object style.

1 From the Slide menu, choose Follow Master, and then choose Background Items.

All the background items, the PowerPoint 3.0 label and the page number, disappear from the slide.

Your presentation window should look similar to the following illustration:

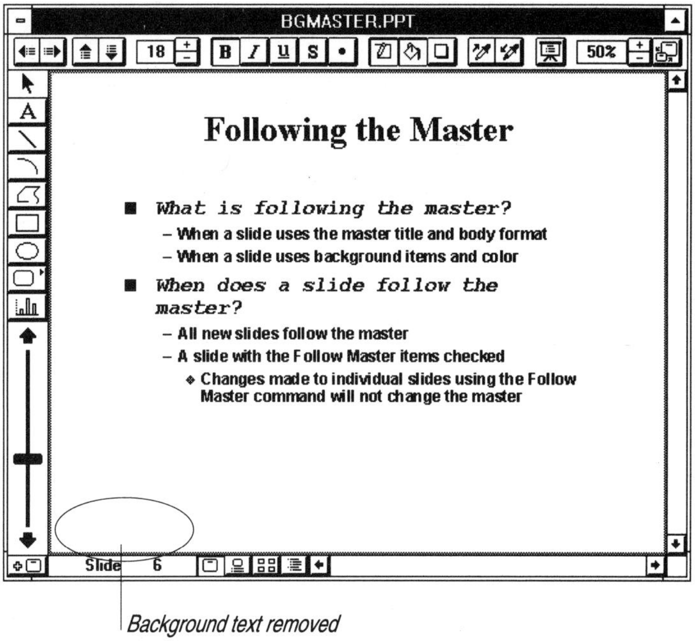

Background text removed

2 From the Slide menu, choose Follow Master, and then choose Background Items.

PowerPoint replaces the missing background items.

Reapply Master

If you make changes to master items on your slide and then decide you want the original master style back, reapply the Slide Master to that slide(s) using the Reapply Master command from the Slide menu. The Reapply Master command reapplies only Slide Master items that are checked in the Follow Master submenu.

1 Click and drag the Title object below the body text.

Your presentation window should look similar to the following illustration:

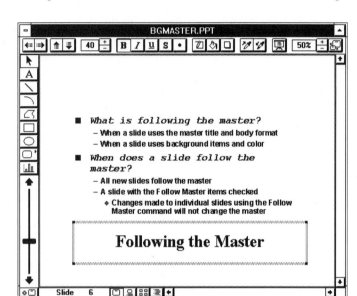

2   From the Slide menu, choose Reapply Master.

PowerPoint uses the Slide Master to reposition the title object to its original position on the slide.

Note   Changes made to the Master view can't be retrieved by using the Reapply Master command.

Change to the next slide

▶ Click the down arrow on the Slide Changer to advance to slide 7.

Customizing PowerPoint Defaults

Default Diamond

A default is the initial attribute setting an object has when it is created. A diamond by a menu item indicates that the attribute is a default setting. To find out the current defaults for your presentation, you can click the Selection Tool and then choose a menu. For example, Bold is a default attribute for text style.

Change text attribute defaults

Selection Tool

1   On the Tool Palette, click the Selection Tool button.

2   From the Text menu, choose Style, and then choose Underline.

Underline is now set as a text default attribute. The Bold text attribute is still set. You have to choose Bold to change the default setting.

Text Tool

3 On the Tool Palette, click the Text Tool button.

4 Position the text cursor in a blank area below the body text and click.

5 Type **Default text is now bold and underlined**.

Selection Tool

6 Click Selection Tool button to deselect the text object.

Change font defaults

1 From the Text menu, choose Font, and then choose Times New Roman.

Note Slide items (Body objects, text objects and any other objects) must not be selected in order for you to set any default settings.

Text Tool

2 On the Tool Palette, click the Text Tool button.

3 Position the text cursor below the text you just typed and click.

4 Type **Times New Roman is now the default font**

Your presentation window should look similar to the following illustration:

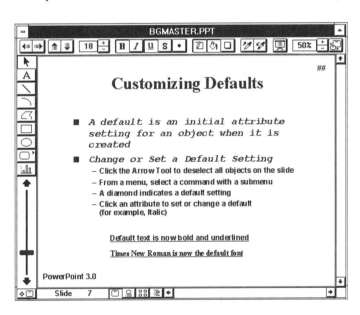

Change to the next slide

▶ Click the down arrow on the Slide Changer to advance to slide 8.

Understanding and Applying Templates

A template can be any PowerPoint presentation. Applying a "template" or presentation to another presentation copies all of the slide, notes, handout, and outline master information to the presentation. A template can be applied to another presentation at any time in the development process, which retroactively applies the Master settings to your presentation. You can apply as many templates as you like until you get the one you like the best.

Change to the next slide

▶ Click the down arrow on the Slide Changer to advance to slide 9.

Apply a Template

1 From the File menu, choose Apply Template.

The Apply Template dialog box appears.

2 In the the Directories box, make sure the PRACTICE directory is open. If it is not, select the drive where the Step by Step practice files are stored and open the appropriate directories.

3 In the list of file names, select TEMPLT05.PPT.

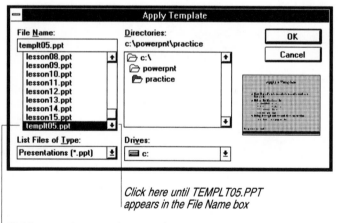

Click here until TEMPLT05.PPT appears in the File Name box

Click here to select a template to apply

4 Click the OK button.

The master information from the Slide, Notes, Handout, and Outline Masters of the template, TEMPLT05.PPT, is applied or copied to the master information in your presentation. The text style and format, color scheme, and background items change to match the template. Your content remains the same.

Your presentation window should look similar to the following illustration:

Print the quick-reference notebook presentation

For information on printing a presentation, refer to Lesson 13.

1   From the File menu, choose Print (CTRL+P).

The Print dialog box appears.

2   Click the down arrow next to the Print box.

3   Click Handouts (2 slides per page) from the drop-down list.

4   Click the OK button.

A dialog box appears to give your printing status.

Save the Presentation

▶   From the File menu, choose Save (CTRL+S).

A dialog box doesn't appear, because the presentation already has a name. The current information in your presentation is saved with the same name.

One Step Further

You have learned how to switch to a master, change the title and body of your presentation, change bullets, adjust margin indents, follow the master, customize PowerPoint defaults, and apply a template. If you'd like to practice these and other basic skills in your practice presentation, try the following:

▶ Change to Notes, Handout, and Outline Master views and add text.

▶ On the Slide Master, change Master Body indents and bullets and see how they effect your presentation.

▶ Change Follow Master settings and change your Slide Master to see how they effect your presentation.

▶ Apply other presentations as a template.

▶ Change other defaults and see how they change your presentation.

If you want to continue to the next lesson

1 From the File menu, choose Close (CTRL+F4).

2 If a dialog box appears asking if you want to save the changes to your presentation, click the No button. You do not need to save the changes you made to the presentation after you printed it.

Choosing this command closes the active presentation; it does not exit PowerPoint. If no other presentations are open, the menu bar displays two available menus: File and Help.

If you want to quit PowerPoint for now

1 From the File menu, choose Exit.

2 If a dialog box appears asking if you want to save changes to the presentation, click the No button.

Lesson Summary

To	Do this
Open Master views	Click the appropriate view button twice or choose the appropriate command from the View menu.
Add background items to a master	Click the appropriate view button twice and add desired items to the master.
Add time, date, and page number	From the Edit menu, choose Insert, and then choose the desired menu item.
Format the Master Title and Body	Select the title or body and choose the desired affects.

To	Do this
Display the text object ruler	From the Text menu, choose Show Ruler.
Set the indent marker for the first line of text	Click and drag the upper triangle.
Set the indent marker for a paragraph other than the first line of text	Click and drag the bottom triangle.
Adjust a paragraph margin	Click and drag the indent marker's midbar.
Create a hanging indent	Position the upper triangle to the left of the bottom triangle.
Change the bullet format	Click the I-beam cursor on a line of text and choose Bullet from the Text menu.
Turn a Follow Master item on or off	From the Slide menu, choose Follow Master, and then choose the appropriate (checked) command.
Reapply the Master to your presentation	From the Slide menu, choose Reapply Master.
Customize default settings	Be sure everything on your slide is deselected, and then from the Object or Text menu choose the item you want to make as the default.
Apply a template	From the File menu, choose Apply Template. Choose the appropriate directory where the template is you want to use, and select the presentation. Click the OK button.

For more information on	See the *Microsoft PowerPoint Handbook*
Masters and Templates	Chapter 5, "Using PowerPoint Masters and Templates"
Rulers and Indent levels	Chapter 8, "Using Special Text Features"

Preview of the Next Lesson

In the next lesson, you'll change a color scheme, change and switch colors, and add colors to menus. By the end of the lesson, you'll have produced another presentation for your quick-reference notebook.

Using a Color Scheme

PowerPoint color schemes are sets of professionally balanced colors designed to be used as the primary colors in your slide presentations. A color scheme consists of eight labeled colors: Background, Lines and Text, Shadows, Title Text, Fills, and three Accent colors. Along with the basic eight basic colors are what PowerPoint calls "Other colors." Other colors will not change when you change a color scheme. You should use one of these colors when the color of an object or picture should never change.

In this lesson, you'll learn how to choose a color scheme, change and switch colors in a color scheme, add a shaded background to a slide, and apply a color scheme to a slide. At the end of the lesson, your presentation will consist of the following slides:

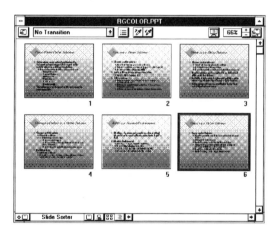

This lesson explains how to do the following:

- View and choose a color scheme
- Change colors in a color scheme
- Add a shaded background
- Add other colors to the menus
- Copy a color scheme

Estimated lesson time: 20 minutes

Open a presentation

If you haven't already started PowerPoint, do so now. For instructions about starting PowerPoint, see "Getting Ready," earlier in this book.

1 From the File menu, choose Open (CTRL+O).

2 In the Directories box, be sure the PRACTICE directory is open. If it is not, select the drive where the Step by Step practice files are stored and open the appropriate directories to find the PRACTICE directory.

For information about opening a sample presentation, refer to Lesson 2.

3 In the list of file names, click LESSON06.PPT.

If you do not see LESSON06.PPT in the list of file names, check to be sure the correct drive and directory are selected. If you need help, see "Getting Ready."

4 Click the OK button.

Your presentation opens to the following slide:

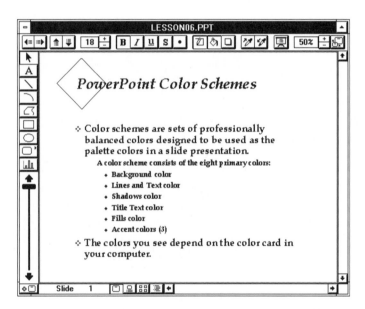

Save the presentation with a new name

Give the presentation a new name so the changes you make in this lesson will not overwrite the original presentation.

1 From the File menu, choose Save As.

2 In the File Name box, type *your initials***color**

For example, if your initials are B. G., type **bgcolor**

3 Click the OK button.

Preview the lesson

The presentation for this lesson contains reference information about PowerPoint colors and color schemes. To preview the information in this lesson, click the Slide Show button on the Toolbar and view the on-screen presentation.

Slide Show

1   On the Toolbar, click the Slide Show button.

PowerPoint displays the first slide in the presentation.

2   Click to advance to the next slide.

3   Click once for each slide to advance through the rest of the presentation.

After the last slide in the presentation, PowerPoint returns to the current view.

Change to the next slide

▶   Click the down arrow on the Slide Changer to advance to slide 2.

Choosing a Color Scheme

PowerPoint comes with sets of professionally designed color combinations that look good together. Every presentation, even a new one, has a color scheme. The color scheme could be a set of custom colors (that you've chosen) or the default color scheme. Understanding color schemes helps you create professional presentations.

Look at a color scheme

1   Click the down arrow on the Slide Changer to advance to slide 3.

2   From the Slide menu, choose Color Scheme.

The Color Scheme dialog box appears, which shows you the colors currently assigned to each of the color slots for your presentation.

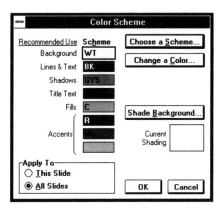

The color scheme for your presentation consists of a Background color, a Lines and Text color, a Shadow color, a Title Text color, a Fills color, and three Accent colors. Each color is placed in a specific slot for a suggested use.

- **Background color**   This color is the canvas color of the slide.

- **Lines and Text color**   This color contrasts with the Background color for writing text and drawing lines.

- **Shadow color**   This color is generally a darker shade of the background.

- **Title Text color**   This color, like the Lines and Text color, contrasts with the Background.

- **Fill color**   This color contrasts with both the Background color and the Line and Text color.

- **Accent colors**   These colors are designed to work as the colors for other objects.

With the color scheme dialog box you can choose a scheme, change a color, shade a background, and apply the color scheme to either the current slide or all the slides in your presentation.

Choose a color scheme

1   Click the Choose a Scheme button.

The Choose a Scheme dialog box appears.

2   Select the Background color WT (white).

A list of colors for Text appears.

3   Select the Text color BK (black).

A list of eight remaining color combinations appears.

4   Select the bottom right set of Remaining Colors.

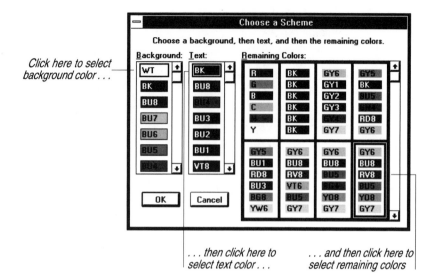

Click here to select
background color . . .

. . . then click here to
select text color . . .

. . . and then click here to
select remaining colors

5   Click the OK button.

The Choose a Scheme dialog box closes, and the Color Scheme dialog box appears with the new scheme colors.

6   Click the OK button.

The new colors apply to all slides.

Change to the next slide

▶   Click the down arrow on the Slide Changer to advance to slide 4.

Changing Colors in a Color Scheme

You can modify any or all of the colors within a color scheme to create your own color combinations. Changes made to a color scheme appear in the Text and Object color menus. As an example, you might want to create a customized color scheme that matches your company's logo. After you have the colors you like, you can simply click and drag a color to a new position or slot in the color scheme to find the best look for your presentation.

Change colors in a color scheme

1   From the Slide menu, choose Color Scheme.

2   Select the accent color YO8.

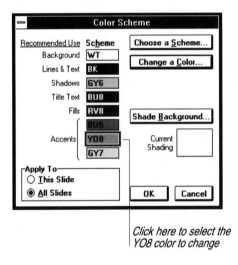

Click here to select the
YO8 color to change

3   Click the Change a Color button.

The Change a Color dialog box appears. The selected color, YO8, appears in the Scheme Color box.

Tip   You can also double-click the color you want to change to go directly to the Change a Color dialog box.

---

4   Select the color BG8 from the color palette.

The Scheme Color changes to BG8.

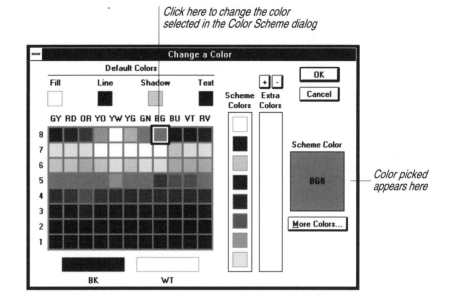

*Click here to change the color
selected in the Color Scheme dialog*

*Color picked
appears here*

Note   To create a custom color, click the More Colors button in the Change a Color dialog box and adjust the Hue, Saturation, and Luminance.

---

5   Click the OK button.

The Accent color changes to BG8.

Switch colors in a color scheme

In the Color Scheme dialog box, you can switch colors in a color scheme by dragging a color to a new slot. (The colors switch positions.)

1   Click and drag the color BG8 up two slots to RV8 (Fills).

BG8 switches positions with RV8.

2   In the Apply To box, click the This Slide option button.

The new color scheme will affect only the current slide.

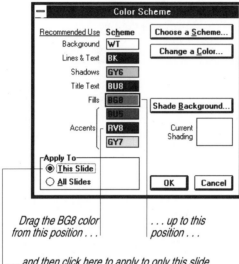

Drag the BG8 color
from this position . . .

. . . up to this
position . . .

. . . and then click here to apply to only this slide

3   Click the OK button.

The new colors are applied to the current slide.

Adding Other Colors to the Menus

You can add extra colors to your color menus in addition to the colors on the color scheme. These are colors you want to remain with the color scheme menu even if the color scheme changes.

Add a color to the menus

1   From the Slide menu, choose Color Scheme.

2   Click the Change a Color button. (You use the same dialog box to add extra colors that you use to change colors).

3   Select the color RD8 from the color palette.

4   Click the Plus (+) button above Extra Colors.

The color RD8 is added to the Extra Colors column of colors.

The Change a Color dialog box should look similar to the following illustration:

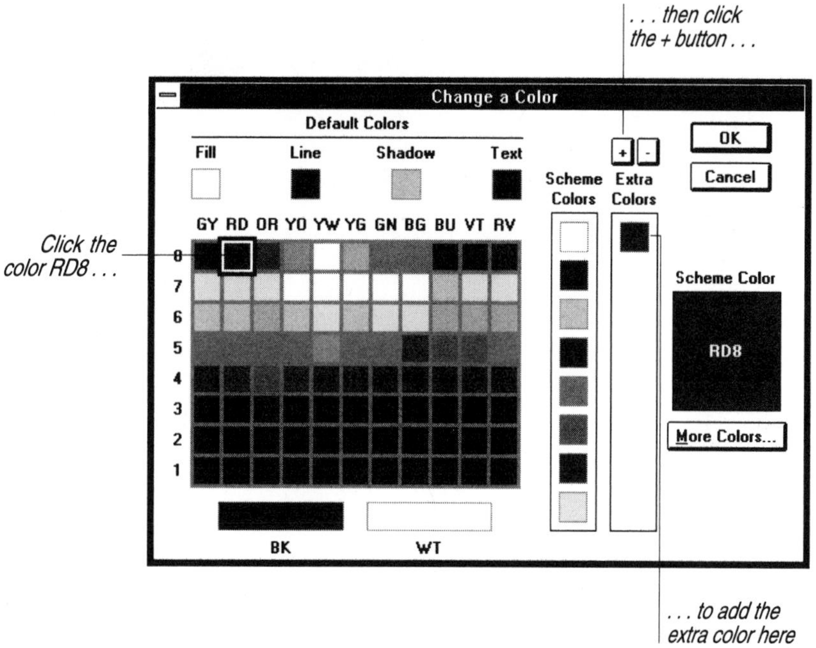

*. . . then click
the + button . . .*

*Click the
color RD8 . . .*

*. . . to add the
extra color here*

Note To delete a certain color from the color scheme menu, select the color from the Extra Colors column and click the Minus (-) button.

5 Click the OK button.

The extra color is added to all the color menus. The Change a Color dialog closes, and the Color Scheme dialog appears. The extra color changes the color scheme.

6 Click the Cancel button.

The color scheme changes are not applied.

Note When a color is added in the Change a Color dialog box, the color selected in the Color Scheme dialog box will also become the added color. To avoid changing the color in the color scheme, click the Cancel button in the Color Scheme dialog box as instructed in step 6 above. The new color will still be added as an "Other Color."

7 From the Object menu, choose Fill.

The Fill submenu appears showing the new color, RD8, added below the Other Color command.

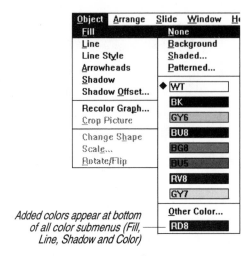

Added colors appear at bottom of all color submenus (Fill, Line, Shadow and Color)

8   Click somewhere off the menu to close the menu.

Change to the next slide

▶   Click the down arrow on the Slide Changer to advance to slide 5.

Adding a Shaded Background

A Shaded background is a visual effect of a solid color gradually changing from light to dark. The shaded background has six different styles, including vertical, horizontal, diagonal right, diagonal left, from corner, and from title. The shading color can be adjusted to make it lighter or darker.

Shade a Background

1   From the Slide menu, choose Color Scheme.

2   Click the Shade Background button.

The Shade Background dialog box appears.

3   In the Shade Styles box, click the Vertical option button.

Four vertical shades appear in the Variants box. The upper left variant appears as the default selection.

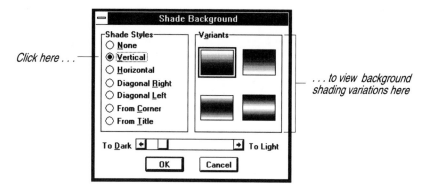

Click here . . .

. . . to view background shading variations here

4   Click the right scroll arrow four or five times to lighten the shade variants.

5   Click the OK button.

The Current Shading box in the Color Scheme dialog box updates with the new shaded background.

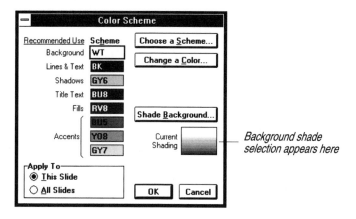

Background shade selection appears here

6   Click the OK button.

The new shaded background applies to the current slide.

Change to the next slide

▶   Click the down arrow on the Slide Changer to advance to slide 6.

Copying a Color Scheme

You can re-use color schemes without having to recreate them. Simply copy or pick up the color scheme from one slide and paste or apply the color scheme to another slide.

Pick up and apply a color scheme

In the Slide Sorter view, the Pick Up and Apply Style buttons on the Toolbar change to Pick Up and Apply Scheme to copy a color scheme from a slide and apply the color scheme to selected slides.

Slide Sorter View

1   Click the Slide Sorter view button.

2   Click slide 5 to select it.

Pick Up Scheme

3   On the Toolbar, click the Pick Up Scheme button.

The color scheme for slide 5 is picked up and is now ready to be applied to other slides in your presentation or any other open presentation.

Note   When you copy a color scheme from one presentation to another, any extra colors on the color scheme menu are not copied.

---

4   From the Edit menu, choose Select All (CTRL+A).

5   On the Toolbar, click the Apply Scheme button.

Apply Scheme

The color scheme applies to all the slides in your presentation.

6   Double-click slide 6.

PowerPoint returns you to Slide view.

Print the quick-reference notebook presentation

For information on printing a presentation, refer to Lesson 13.

1   From the File menu, choose Print (CTRL+P).

The Print dialog box appears.

2   Click the down arrow next to the Print box.

3   Select Handouts (2 slides per page) from the drop-down list.

4   Click the OK button.

A dialog box appears to give your printing status.

Save the Presentation

▶   From the File menu, choose Save (CTRL+S).

A dialog box doesn't appear, because the presentation already has a name. The current information in your presentation is saved with the same name.

One Step Further

You have learned to view a color scheme, choose a color scheme, change a color and add extra colors to color menus, add a shaded background, and copy a color scheme. If you'd like to practice these and other basic skills in your practice presentation, try the following:

▶ Add shaded backgrounds with different shade styles such as Diagonal, Right or Left, From Corner or From Title and change the lightness and darkness of the shade.

▶ Create a custom color and add it to the color menus.

▶ Use the Pick Up Scheme command from a different presentation to copy a color scheme and the Apply Scheme command to paste the color scheme into your presentation.

If you want to continue to the next lesson

1   From the File menu, choose Close (CTRL+F4).

2   If a dialog box appears asking whether you want to save the changes to your presentation, click the No button. You do not need to save the changes you made to the presentation after you printed it.

Choosing this command closes the active presentation; it does not exit PowerPoint. If no other presentations are open, the menu bar displays two available menus: File and Help.

If you want to quit PowerPoint for now

1   From the File menu, choose Exit.

2   If a dialog box appears asking if you want to save changes to the presentation, click the No button.

Lesson Summary

To	Do this
View a color scheme	From the Slide menu, choose Color Scheme.
Choose a color scheme	From the Color Scheme dialog box, click the Choose a Scheme button. Click a Background color, Text color, and a set of Remaining Colors.
Change a color in a color scheme	From the Color Scheme dialog box, select a color from color scheme. Click the Change a Color button. Select a new color.
Switch a color in a color scheme	From the Color Scheme dialog box, click and drag the color to a new location.
Add other colors to the menus	From the Color Scheme dialog box, click the Change a Color button. Select a color. Click the Plus (+) button.
Add a shaded background	From the Color Scheme dialog box, click the Shade Background button. Select a Shade Style and Variant.
Copy a color scheme	From the Slide Sorter view, select a slide with the color scheme you want. On the Toolbar, click the Pick Up Scheme button. Select the slide(s). On the Toolbar, click the Apply Scheme button.

For more information on	See the *Microsoft PowerPoint Handbook*
Color Schemes	Chapter 6, "Working with Color Schemes"

Preview of the Next Lesson

In the next lesson, you'll draw shapes, arcs and freeforms, edit and modify objects, move and group objects. At the end of the lesson, you'll have another presentation for your quick-reference notebook.

Drawing and Modifying Objects

With PowerPoint's drawing features, you can draw and modify shapes, lines, text, and pictures to create professional-looking images. Objects are the building blocks you use to create slides in PowerPoint. The shapes you draw, the pictures you import from other applications, the text you type—these are all objects.

In this lesson, you'll draw and edit objects, change object attributes, group and ungroup objects, draw and edit arcs and freeforms, and rotate and flip objects. At the end of the lesson, your presentation will consist of the following slides:

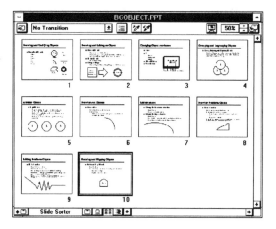

This lesson explains how to do the following:

- Draw and edit objects
- Modify object attributes
- Group and ungroup objects
- Align objects
- Draw and edit arc and freeform objects
- Rotate and flip objects

Estimated lesson time: 50 minutes

Open a presentation

If you haven't already started PowerPoint, do so now. For instructions about starting PowerPoint, see "Getting Ready," earlier in this book.

1 From the File menu, choose Open (CTRL+O).

2 In the Directories box, be sure the PRACTICE directory is open. If it is not, select the drive where the Step by Step practice files are stored and open the appropriate directories to find the PRACTICE directory.

For information about opening a sample presentation, refer to Lesson 2.

3 In the list of file names, select LESSON07.PPT.

If you do not see LESSON07.PPT in the list of file names, check to be sure the correct drive and directory are selected. If you need help, see "Getting Ready."

4 Click the OK button.

Your presentation opens to the following slide:

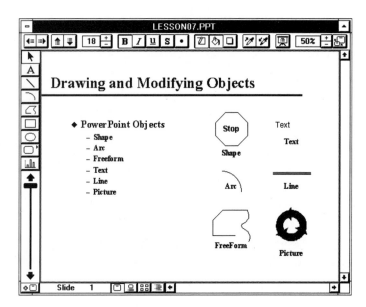

Save the presentation with a new name

Give the presentation a new name so the changes you make in this lesson will not overwrite the original presentation.

1 From the File menu, choose Save As.

2 In the File Name box, type y*our initials***object**

For example, if your initials are B. G., type **bgobject**

3 Click the OK button.

Preview the lesson

The presentation for this lesson contains reference information about drawing and modifying objects in PowerPoint. To preview the information in this lesson, click the Slide Show button on the Toolbar and view the on-screen presentation.

Slide Show

1   On the Toolbar, click the Slide Show button.

PowerPoint displays the first slide in the presentation.

2   Click to advance to the next slide.

3   Click once for each slide to advance through the rest of the presentation.

After the last slide in the presentation, PowerPoint returns to the current view.

Working with Objects

Objects are shapes, lines, text, and pictures that you create or insert into your PowerPoint presentation. You can create objects with the text and drawing tools on the Tool Palette. An object has graphic attributes (fill, line, shape, and shadow) and text attributes (style, font, color, emboss, and shadow).

Selecting and Deselecting Objects

To select an object, click a visible part of the object using the Selection Tool button on the Tool Palette. Deselect an object by clicking the Selection Tool button or move your pointer off the object into a blank area of the slide and click. You can apply attributes only to objects you've selected.

Select and deselect an object

Selection Tool

1   On the Tool Palette, click the Selection Tool button. (It should already be selected unless you've clicked another tool from the Tool Palette.)

2   Position your pointer on any part of the text object entitled "PowerPoint Objects" and click.

The text object is surrounded by a fuzzy outline called a *selection box* that indicates the object is selected. The black squares at each corner of the object are resize handles used to resize objects.

3   Click outside the selection box in a blank area of the slide.

The object deselects.

Select and deselect multiple objects

You can select and deselect more than one object in different ways. One method uses the SHIFT key and the mouse.

1   Select the "Text" object with the gray frame.

2   Press and hold the SHIFT key, and then click the "Stop" object.

The "Text" object remains selected, and the "Stop" object is added to the selection. For multiple selections, the resize handles do not appear. As long as you hold down the SHIFT key while clicking unselected objects, you continually add objects to the selection.

3   Press and hold the SHIFT key, and then click the "Stop" object again.

The "Stop" object is removed from the selection.

Tip   You can also draw a selection box by clicking and dragging the pointer around more than one object to select them.

Change to the next slide

▶   Click the down arrow on the Slide Changer to advance to slide 2.

Drawing an Object

All objects in PowerPoint, except freeforms, are created using the same technique. Select a tool from the Tool Palette and then click and drag your mouse. Using the SHIFT key as you drag allows you to draw squares and circles. Using the CTRL key as you drag allows you to draw from the center outward.

Shape Tool

1   On the Tool Palette, click and hold the Shape Tool button until the pop-out menu appears.

Note   Your Shape tool on the Tool Palette might look different depending on the last shape selected.

---

2   Select the Right Arrow in the second from the bottom row.

Your Shape menu should look similar to the one in the following illustration:

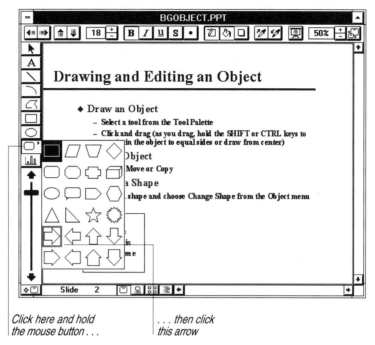

Click here and hold
the mouse button . . .

. . . then click
this arrow

3   Position the cross hairs cursor right of the text rectangle and then click and drag.

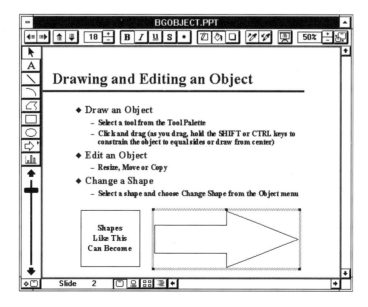

4   Click outside the selection box in a blank area to deselect the arrow object.

Note   When you draw an object, PowerPoint uses its default settings, such as line style, or fill color. For more information, see "Customizing PowerPoint Defaults" in Lesson 5, "Changing Masters and Applying Templates."

Editing an Object

Resizing, copying, pasting, moving, cutting, and deleting are editing commands you can use on objects. To edit a PowerPoint object, select it, and then choose a command from a menu or the Toolbar.

Resize an object

Often you'll draw an object or import a picture that won't be the right size for your presentation. Change the size of an object by dragging the resize handles.

1   Select the arrow object.

2   Click and drag the arrow's upper right resize handle to the left to match the following illustration:

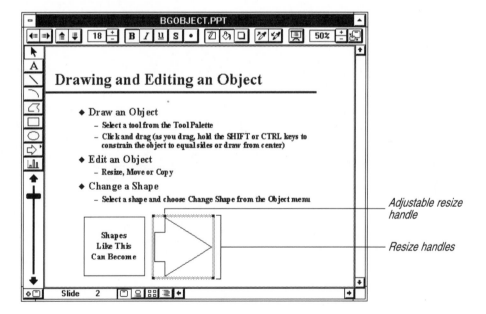

Adjustable resize handle

Resize handles

Tip   Holding down the SHIFT or CTRL keys while you drag a resize handle controls the sizing of the object. Drag+SHIFT resizes the object vertically, horizontally or diagonally. Drag+CTRL resizes the object from the center outward. Drag+CTRL+SHIFT resizes the object proportionally from the object's center outward.

Adjust an object

Some PowerPoint objects, such as traingles, parallelograms, and rounded rectangles, are adjustable. Adjustable objects also have a fifth resize handle positioned on one side of the object in between two corner resize handles.

▶   Click and drag the arrow's adjustable resize handle to the left as shown in the following illustration:

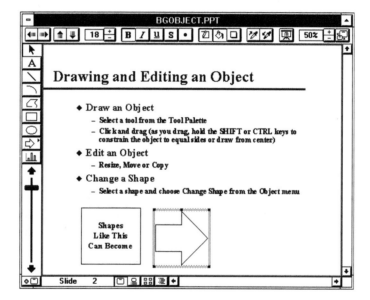

Copy an object

PowerPoint copies the currently selected objects to the Windows Clipboard. You can paste the objects in other parts of your presentation.

1   From the Edit menu, choose Copy (CTRL+C).

The arrow is copied to the Windows Clipboard.

2   From the Edit menu, choose Paste (CTRL+V).

A copy of the arrow is pasted to the slide from the Windows Clipboard. The pasted arrow is selected and overlaps the original arrow.

Your presentation window should look similar to the following illustration:

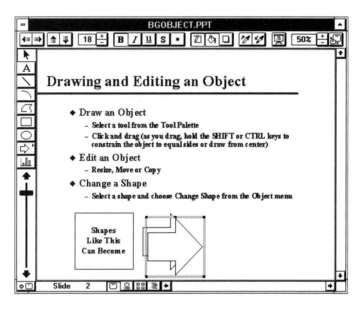

Move an object

1   Position your pointer over the new arrow object.

2   Click and drag the new arrow to the right of the original arrow.

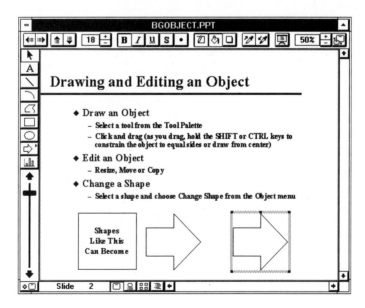

Tip You can copy and move an object in one step. Hold the CTRL key, and click and drag an object to duplicate it. Choose Duplicate Again from the Edit menu to easily create another copy of the object with the same drag distance as the first.

Change the shape of an object

PowerPoint allows you to change an existing shape to another shape with one easy command.

1 From the Object menu, choose Change Shape.

The Shape submenu appears.

2 Select the starburst shape from the pop-out submenu.

The arrow changes to the starburst shape. The new starburst shape fits in the same area and keeps the same attributes as the original arrow shape.

Your presentation window should look similar to the following illustration:

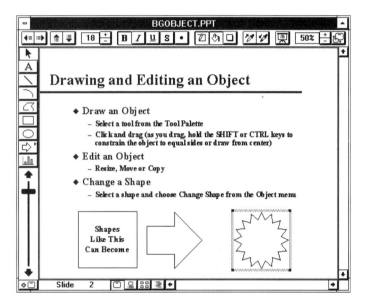

Add text to an object

When you add text to an object, PowerPoint automatically centers the text as you type. When you want to start a new line, you can press ENTER.

1 Type **Great!**

2 Click outside the object to deselect the object.

Change to the next slide

▶ Click the down arrow on the Slide Changer to advance to slide 3.

Modifying Object Attributes

Objects have attributes that define how they appear on the slide. An object has graphic attributes such as fill, line, shape, and shadow, and text attributes such as style, font, color, emboss, and shadow.

Add and modify object frame

1 Select the object entitled "PowerPoint Object."

Frame

2 On the Toolbar, click the Frame button.

The default line color and style appear around the object.

3 From the Object menu, choose Line Style, and then choose the thickest line (fifth from the bottom).

The line style changes to a thick line.

4 From the Object menu, choose line, and then choose Blue (B).

Your presentation window should look similar to the following illustration:

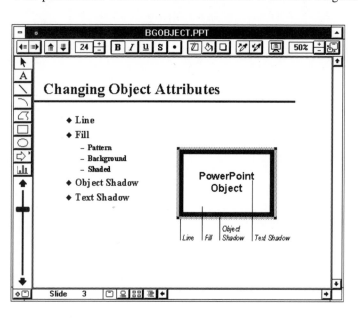

Add and modify object fill

1 From the Object menu, choose Fill, and then choose Patterned.

The Patterned Fill dialog box appears. (If the dialog box covers the object you've selected, click and drag the dialog Title bar to move the dialog box.)

2 Select the second pattern in the first row.

Click this pattern

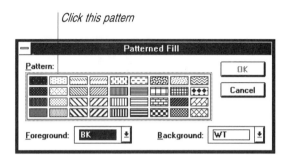

The dotted pattern applies to the object so you can see how the pattern will look before closing the dialog box.

3 Click the OK button.

4 From the Object menu, choose Fill, and then choose the color GY6.

The object fills with the gray color GY6, replacing the dotted pattern.

Add and modify object shadow

Object Shadow

1 On the Toolbar, click the Object Shadow button.

The default shadow color GY3 appears around the object entitled "PowerPoint Object."

2 From the Object menu, choose Shadow Offset.

The Shadow Offset dialog box appears.

3 Click the Left option button.

The object's shadow changes to the left, allowing you to see how the shadow change will look before leaving the dialog box.

4 Click the up arrow in the lower Points box to 15.

5 Click the up arrow in the upper Points box to 15.

The Shadow Offset dialog box should look similar to the following:

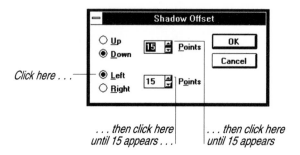

The shadow offset is applied to the object so you can see the shadow change before leaving the dialog box.

6 Click the OK button.

Add shadow to text

▶ From the Text menu, choose Style and then choose Shadow.

A white text shadow appears.

Change to the next slide

▶ Click the down arrow on the Slide Changer to advance to slide 4.

Grouping and Ungrouping Objects

Objects can be grouped together, ungrouped, and regrouped in PowerPoint to make editing and moving information easier. Grouped objects appear as one object, but maintain their individual attributes. You can change an individual object within a group of objects by ungrouping them and making the change. Group the objects together again by choosing the Regroup command.

Group objects

1 Click and drag a selection box around the three circles on slide 4.

Each circle has its own selection box, as shown in the following illustration:

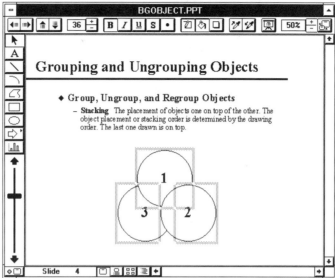

2 From the Arrange menu, choose Group (CTRL+G).

The three circle objects group together as one object, as shown in the following illustration:

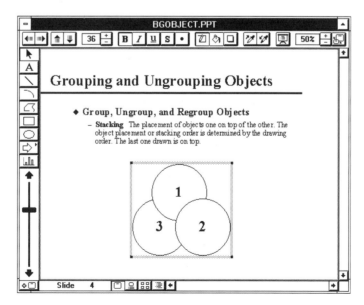

Ungroup objects

1   From the Arrange menu, choose Ungroup (CTRL+H).

2   Click outside the selection box to deselect the grouped object.

Object stacking order

Stacking is the placement of an object one on top of another. The drawing order determines the object stacking order. The first object you draw is on the bottom, while the last object you draw is on top. You can change the placement of the objects by using the Bring to Front, Send to Back, Bring Forward, or Send Backward commands on the Arrange menu.

1   Click circle 1 to select it.

2   From the Arrange menu, choose Send Backward (CTRL+-).

Circle 1 moves down one level on the stack of objects.

3   From the Arrange menu, choose Bring to Front.

Circle 1 moves to the top of the stack of circle objects.

Regroup objects

Objects previously grouped can be regrouped in one easy step. After you ungroup a set of objects, PowerPoint remembers each object in the group and automatically regroups the objects with the Regroup command.

▶   From the Arrange menu, choose Regroup (CTRL+J).

The three circles regroup.

Note   PowerPoint remembers the objects in a group so you don't have to select the objects to regroup them.

Change to the next slide

▶   Click the down arrow on the Slide Changer to advance to slide 5.

Aligning Objects

Objects can be aligned vertically or horizontally using the Align command or the PowerPoint guides. The Align command aligns two or more objects relative to each other vertically to the left, to the center, or to the right. You can also align objects horizontally to the top, to the middle, or to the bottom. The PowerPoint guides align an individual or group of objects to a vertical or horizontal straight edge. For exact alignment, turn on Snap to Grid, an invisible grid of evenly spaced lines that helps align objects.

Align objects with guides

1   From the Arrange menu, choose Show Guides (CTRL+Y).

Vertical and horizontal dotted lines appear, indicating the guides are turned on.

2   Move your pointer and position it on the vertical guide.

3   Click and drag the guide left to position 1.00.

The pointer changes to a number indicating inches left or right from the slide center.

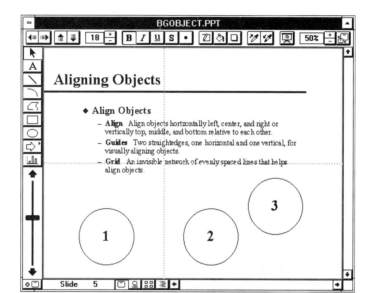

4   Click and drag circle 2 left to the vertical guide.

As the circle approaches the guide, the object snaps to the guide.

5   From the Arrange menu, choose Show Guides.

The Show Guides command turns off.

Align an object

1   Select all three circles.

2   From the Arrange menu, choose Align and then choose Middles.

The circle objects align horizontally to each other in the middle, as shown in the following illustration:

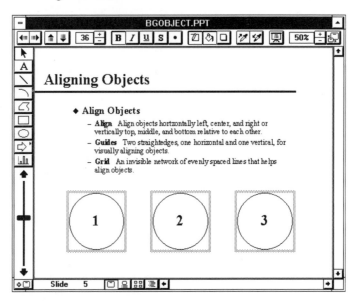

Change to the next slide

▶ Click the down arrow on the Slide Changer to advance to slide 6.

Drawing and Editing an Arc

With PowerPoint, you can draw and edit arcs of all sizes and shapes. You can change the shape of any arc by resizing it or moving its control handles. The direction in which you drag the arc determines whether the arc opens up or down, and the distance you drag the arc determines its size.

Draw an arc

Arc Tool

1 On the Tool Palette, click the Arc Tool button.

The pointer changes to a cross hairs cursor.

2 Position the cross hairs cursor under the center of the Body object.

3 Hold the SHIFT key down and drag the cross hairs cursor down to the right.

Your presentation window should look similar to the following illustration:

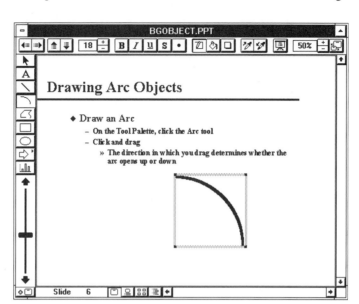

Note   You can't attach text to lines, arcs, and freeforms like you can with other objects. Lines, arcs, and freeforms can't be changed using the Shape command.

Change to the next slide

▶ Click the down arrow on the Slide Changer to advance to slide 7.

Edit the roundness of an arc

1   Position your pointer on the arc line and click to select the arc.

2   Click and drag the upper left resize handle to the left.

As the arc changes, a dotted outline of the arc displays indicating to you the new size when you release the mouse button.

Your presentation window should look similar to the following illustration:

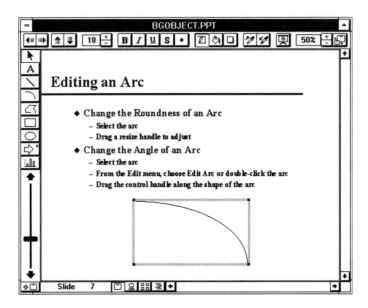

Edit the angle of an arc

1 From the Edit menu, choose Edit Arc (CTRL+E) or double-click the arc line.

A control handle appears on either end of the arc as shown in the following illustration:

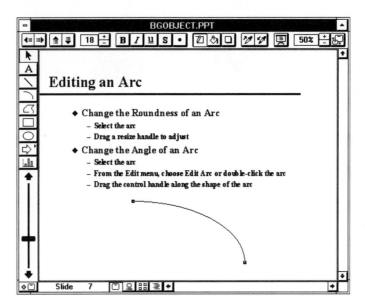

2   Click and drag the left control handle to the left.

Your slide should look similar to the following illustration:

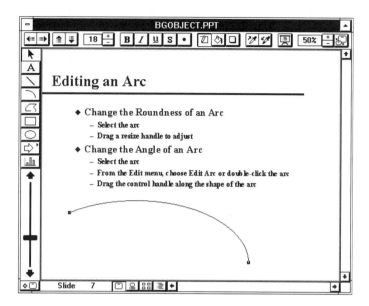

Change to the next slide

▶   Click the down arrow on the Slide Changer to advance to slide 8.

Drawing and Editing a Freeform Object

A freeform object can consist of straight lines, freehand lines, or a combination of the two. Freeform objects can be closed or open. A closed freeform has the end of its last line connected to the beginning of its first line, and an open freeform is not connected.

Drawing a Freeform Object

Freeform Tool

1   On the Tool Palette, click the Freeform Tool button.

2   Position your cursor just below the body text in the center.

The pointer changes to a cross hairs cursor.

Drawing with the Freeform tool allows you to draw straight lines and freehand lines. You can switch back and forth between the pencil (freehand) and the cross hairs (straight line) cursors by holding and releasing the mouse button.

3 Click once.

This sets the freeform starting point. *Don't hold down the mouse button while you draw.*

4 Move the cross hairs cursor down the slide about 1.5 inches to a new position and click once.

5 Move your cross hairs cursor to the left about 2 inches.

Tip To delete the last line of a freeform object while you're drawing, press the BACKSPACE key. You can delete all but the first point this way.

---

6 Hold down the mouse button and draw a line with the pencil to the freeform object's starting point and click once. (The pencil cursor follows your mouse movements.)

Your slide should look similar to the following illustration:

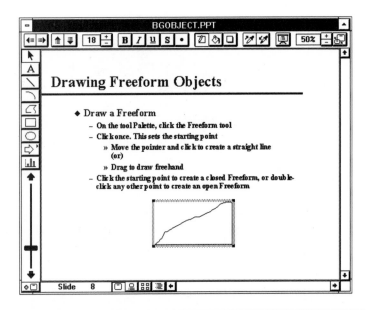

Note To create an open freeform, double-click the last point of your freeform without connecting the object's ends.

Change to the next slide

▶ Click the down arrow on the Slide Changer to advance to slide 9.

Editing a Freeform Object

Editing a freeform object involves moving, adding, or deleting any of a freeform object's points. What appears to be the curved lines of a freeform are really just a series of very short straight lines connected to one another.

Adjust a vertex

1 Double-click a freeform line to edit a freeform object.

Your presentation window should look similar to the following illustration:

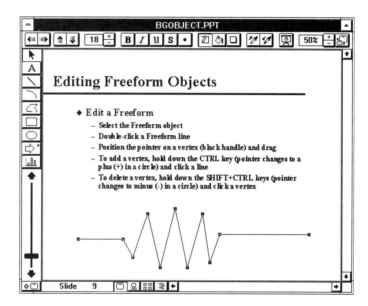

You're now in edit mode. In edit mode all of the freeform points, called vertices, appear and the pointer becomes a black arrow. Now you can edit the freeform object by moving vertices, adding vertices, or deleting vertices.

2 Click and drag the left vertex to a new position on the slide.

As you click and drag, the black arrow changes to a white arrow. As you move the vertex, a dotted outline displays to show you the new position when you release the mouse button.

Add a vertex

▶ Hold down the CTRL key and click the between the first two vertices on the line.

When you hold down the CTRL key, the black arrow cursor changes to a circle with a plus sign (+) in the middle.

Subtract a vertex

1 Hold down the CTRL and SHIFT keys and click the cursor on the vertex you just added to the freeform.

When you hold down the CTRL and SHIFT keys, the black arrow cursor changes to a circle with a (-) sign in the middle. The vertex you added in the last step is deleted.

2 Deselect the freeform object.

Change to the next slide

▶ Click the down arrow on the Slide Changer to advance to slide 10.

Rotating and Flipping Objects

1 Select the "Home" object.

2 From the Object menu, choose Rotate/Flip, and then choose Rotate Right.

The shape rotates to the right.

Note   Text, patterns, shadows and bitmaps don't rotate or flip.

Your presentation window should look similar to the following illustration:

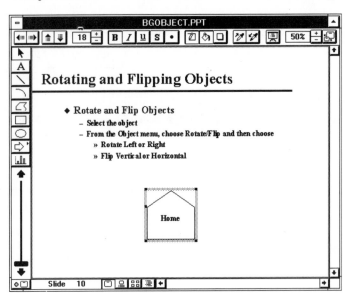

Print the quick-reference notebook presentation

For information on printing a presentation, refer to Lesson 13.

1   From the File menu, choose Print (CTRL+P).

   The Print dialog box appears.

2   Click the down arrow next to the Print box.

3   Select Handouts (2 slides per page) from the drop-down list.

4   Click the OK button.

   A dialog box appears to give your printing status.

Save the Presentation

▶   From the File menu, choose Save (CTRL+S).

   A dialog box doesn't appear, because the presentation already has a name. The current information in your presentation is saved with the same name.

One Step Further

You have learned to select and deselect objects, draw and modify objects, draw arcs and freeforms, align, group, upgroup, rotate, and flip objects. If you'd like to practice these and other basic skills in your practice presentation, try the following:

▶   Change the fill of an object to shaded.

▶   Draw lines, change line styles, and add arrowheads.

▶   Copy and move an object using the Duplicate command.

▶   Group, ungroup, and regroup different types of objects.

▶   Align objects with the different vertical and horizontal alignment types.

▶   Draw and edit arcs and freeform objects.

If you want to continue to the next lesson

1   From the File menu, choose Close (CTRL+F4).

2   If a dialog box appears asking whether you want to save the changes made to the presentation, click the No button. You do not need to save the changes you made to the presentation after you printed it.

   Choosing this command closes the active presentation; it does not exit PowerPoint. If no other presentations are open, the menu bar displays two available menus: File and Help.

If you want to quit PowerPoint for now

1   From the File menu, choose Exit.

2   If a dialog box appears asking if you want to save changes to the presentation, click the No button.

Lesson Summary

To	Do this
Select an object	Click the Selection Tool button. Position the cursor on the object and click.
Deselect an object	Click the Selection Tool button.
Draw an object	Click a drawing tool from the Tool Palette and drag.
Resize an object	Select the object. Click and drag a resize handle.
Change an object's shape	Select the shape. From the Object menu, choose Change Shape.
Change a frame	From the Object menu, choose Line Style, and then choose a line type.
Group or Ungroup objects	Select the object(s). From the Arrange menu, choose Group or Ungroup.
Align objects	Select the objects. From the Arrange menu, choose Align, and then choose an alignment, or Show Guides and align.
Draw an arc	On the Tool Palette, click the Arc Tool button and drag.
Edit an arc	Select the arc. Double-click the arc line. Click and drag control handles.
Draw a freeform	On the Tool Palette, click the Freeform Tool button. Click, position mouse, and click, or click and drag the mouse.
Edit a freeform	Select the freeform. Double-click a freeform line. Click and drag vertices.
Rotate and flip objects	Select the object. From the Object menu choose Rotate/Flip.

For more information on	See the *Microsoft PowerPoint Handbook*
PowerPoint Objects	Chapter 4, "Working with PowerPoint Objects"
Drawing in PowerPoint	Chapter 10, "Drawing"

Preview of the Next Lesson

In the next lesson, you'll create and edit a graph. By the end of the lesson, you'll have produced another presentation for your quick-reference notebook.

4 Adding Graphs

Creating a Graph

To create graphs on your slides, PowerPoint uses an embedded application called Microsoft Graph. Graph utilizes many of the same features of Microsoft Excel. Adding graphs to a presentation can help communicate your ideas in an effective, professional manner.

When you create a graph with Microsoft Graph and return to your presentation slide, the graph becomes an *embedded object*. An embedded object maintains a "link" with its original application for easy editing. For more information on embedding, see Lesson 12, "Linking Information with Other Applications."

In this lesson, you'll learn how to start Graph from PowerPoint, create a graph, use basic features of Graph, return to your presentation, and edit your graph from PowerPoint. At the end of the lesson, your presentation will consist of the following slides:

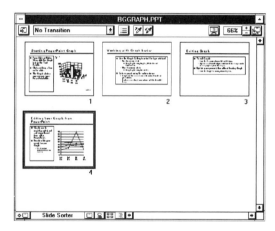

This lesson explains how to do the following:

- Start Graph using the Graph tool
- Create a graph
- Use basic Graph features
- Exit Graph
- Edit Graph from within PowerPoint

Estimated lesson time: 20 minutes

Open a presentation

If you haven't already started PowerPoint, do so now. For instructions about starting PowerPoint, see "Getting Ready," earlier in this book.

1 From the File menu, choose Open (CTRL+O).

2 In the Directories box, be sure the PRACTICE directory is open. If it is not, select the drive where the Step by Step practice files are stored and open the appropriate directories to find the PRACTICE directory.

For information about opening a sample presentation, refer to Lesson 2.

3 In the list of file names, click LESSON08.PPT.

If you do not see LESSON08.PPT in the list of file names, check to be sure the correct drive and directory are selected. If you need help, see "Getting Ready."

4 Click the OK button.

Your presentation opens to the following slide:

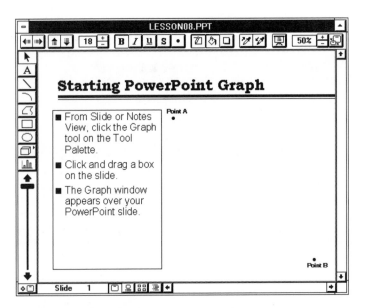

Save the presentation with a new name

Give the presentation a new name so the changes you make in this lesson will not overwrite the original document.

1 From the File menu, choose Save As.

2 In the File Name box, type *your initials***graph**

For example, if your initials are B.G., type **bggraph**

3 Click the OK button.

Preview the lesson

The presentation for this lesson contains reference information about graphing in PowerPoint. To preview the information in this lesson, click the Slide Show button on the Toolbar and view the on-screen presentation.

Slide Show

1 On the Toolbar, click the Slide Show button.

PowerPoint displays the first slide in the presentation.

2 Click to advance to the next slide.

3 Click once for each slide to advance through the rest of the presentation.

After the last slide in the presentation, PowerPoint returns to the current view.

Starting Graph

Microsoft Graph is a separate application that PowerPoint uses to embed graph objects on your presentation slide. You can start Graph using the Graph tool on the Tool Palette or choosing Insert Object from the Edit menu. Starting Graph creates an embedded graph object you can edit later.

Graph Tool

The size of box you draw will determine the size of your graph.

1 On the Tool Palette, click the Graph Tool and then position the pointer on the slide.

2 Click and drag to make a box between point A and point B on your slide.

PowerPoint creates a placeholder for Graph and launches the embedded application Microsoft Graph. A Graph Datasheet and Chart appear.

	1st Qtr	2nd Qtr	3rd Qtr	4th Qtr
East				20.4
West				31.6
North				43.9

Graph Datasheet window   *Graph Chart window*

The chart window displayed in the Graph window represents the graph that will be embedded in your PowerPoint presentation. Changes made to your datasheet appear on this graph. The chart window is a graphical representation of the information in the datasheet. The datasheet and chart appear with default data and can be modified to meet your specific needs.

Note   If the Microsoft Graph default settings have been altered, the Graph Chart and Datasheet will not look like the above Graph window.

Working with Graph Basics

The basics of Graph design include format, shape and color. The appropriate graph format and color will enhance your presentation's message and communicate your ideas powerfully.

Graph Gallery

The Graph Gallery allows you to choose the format for your graph. There are 12 graph categories, including two-dimensional graphs and three-dimensional graphs, for a total of 84 different formats.

The Gallery menu is divided into two sections; seven 2-D formats and five 3-D formats.

1   From the Gallery menu, choose 3-D Pie.

The Chart Gallery dialog box appears displaying seven different three-dimensional (3-D) Pie formats.

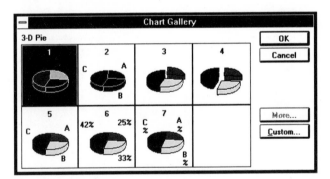

2   Click format number 4.

3   Click the OK button.

Your graph window should look similar to the following illustration:

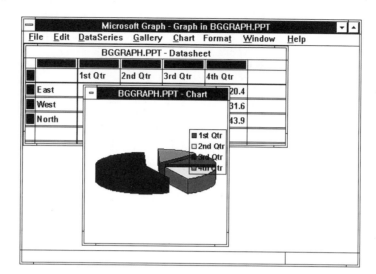

Changing the graph's format repositions the legend so it overlays the 3-D pie.

For information on working with legends, refer to Lesson 10.

4 From the Chart menu, choose Delete Legend.

Graph removes the legend from your graph.

5 From the Gallery menu, choose Pie.

Seven different two-dimensional (2-D) pie graph formats appear.

6 Select format number 4, if it is not already selected.

7 Click the OK button.

Your graph window should look similar to the following illustration:

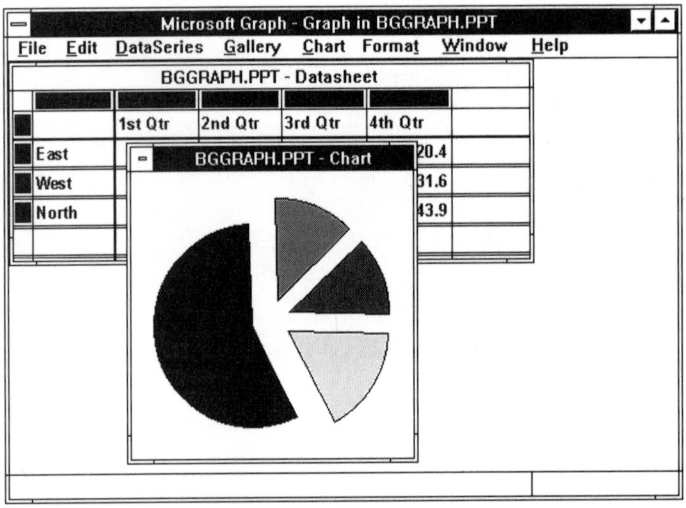

Practice for a moment

- From the Gallery menu, choose different 2-D and 3-D graph formats.
- Select different views and see how they affect your graph.
- When you are finished, from the Gallery menu, choose 3-D Column, select format 6, and click the OK button.

Graph color

The color scheme of the active PowerPoint presentation determines the Graph color scheme.

To view the PowerPoint color scheme dialog box, refer to Lesson 6.

PowerPoint Color Scheme	Graph Color Scheme
Background	Graph background
Lines and Text	Axes, gridlines and text
Fills	First item in the color series
Accents	Second, third, and fourth items in the color series
Shadows	Fifth item in the color series
Title Text	Sixth item in the color series

1 From the Format menu, choose Color Palette.

The Color Palette dialog box appears.

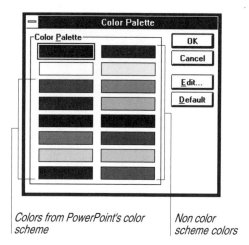

Colors from PowerPoint's color scheme | Non color scheme colors

The Graph color scheme displayed in the left column of the dialog box is the color scheme from the active PowerPoint presentation. The top color in the column is used for line separators on pie wedges and bar columns and is best left black. The second color in the column is used for patterned fills and generally works best left white. The remaining colors in the left column correspond to various colors in the PowerPoint color scheme.

2 Click the third color box from the top in the left column.

A blinking cursor appears underneath the color box.

3 Click the Edit button.

The Graph color editing box appears.

Tip Double-clicking any color box in the Color Palette dialog box will activate the color editing box.

---

4   Move the pointer to any color on the color box and click.

The color in the Color|Solid box changes to the color you chose.

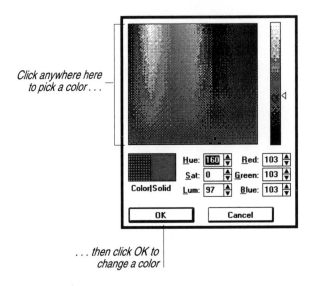

Click anywhere here to pick a color . . .

. . . then click OK to change a color

5   Click the OK button.

The Color Palette dialog box appears. The color in the selected color box changes.

6   Click the OK button.

The data series color changes to the color picked in the color editing box.

Exiting Graph

When exiting Graph, you can either update your presentation with changes you've made or ignore the changes. You can also update your presentation with changes you've made to a graph without exiting Graph.

Exit Graph and update your presentation

1   From the File menu, choose Exit and Return to BGGRAPH.PPT.

A Microsoft Graph dialog box appears.

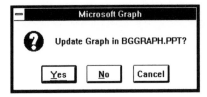

2 Click the Yes button to update your presentation.

Microsoft Graph places the graph on your slide where you drew the graph box.

Note If you wish to update your PowerPoint presentation and continue to work in Graph, choose Update from the File menu. This will position your graph on the slide and let you make additional changes while still working in Graph.

Editing a Graph from PowerPoint

For information on editing objects, refer to Lesson 7.

After you have created a graph on your PowerPoint slide, you can edit it much like other objects. You can move graphs on the slide to accommodate other objects on the slide. You can cut, copy, paste and reposition graphs from one PowerPoint slide to another or from one presentation to another.

Reposition the graph on the slide

1 Click and drag the graph to a different position on the slide.

2 Click and drag the graph back to its original position.

Cut, copy, and paste a graph

1 From the Edit menu choose Copy (CTRL+C).

TROUBLESHOOTING:

If the Copy command is dimmed Check to be sure the graph is selected. Click on the graph to select it.

Slide Changer

2 Click the down arrow on the Slide Changer until slide 4 displays.

3 From the Edit menu, choose Paste (CTRL+V)

Graph pastes a duplicate graph onto slide 4.

4 Click the up arrow on the Slide Changer to move to slide 1.

5 Move the pointer onto the graph and click to select it.

6 Press DELETE.

The graph deletes from slide 1.

7 From the Edit menu, choose Paste.

Graph returns the graph to slide 1.

You can move graphs within the same presentation or to other presentations by cutting and pasting or by copying and pasting.

Edit your graph from PowerPoint

You can edit your graph from PowerPoint by double-clicking the graph.

1 Click the down arrow on the Slide Changer to move to slide 4.

2 Double-click the graph.

The Graph window appears.

3 From the Gallery menu, choose Line.

Eight available line graph formats appear.

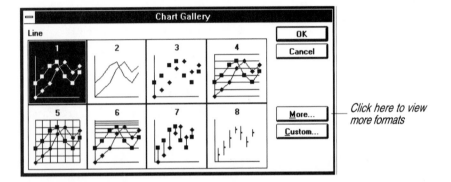

Click here to view
more formats

Some graph formats have more than eight different formats. You can view additional formats by clicking the More button if it is not dimmed.

4 Click the More button.

One additional line graph format appears.

5 Click the More button again.

The first eight line graph formats reappear.

6 Click format number 4.

7 Click the OK button.

8 From the File menu, choose Exit and Return.

9 Click the Yes button on the Microsoft Graph update dialog box.

Your presentation window should look similar to the following illustration:

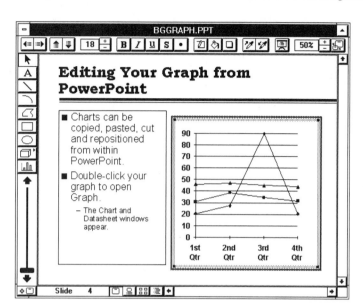

Print the quick-reference notebook presentation

Print this lesson of your quick-reference notebook in handout pages.

For information on printing a presentation, refer to Lesson 13.

1   From the File menu, choose Print (CTRL+P).

The Print dialog box appears.

2   Click the down arrow next to the Print box.

3   Click Handouts (2 slides per page) form the drop-down list.

4   Click the OK button.

A dialog box appears to give your printing status.

Save the presentation

To save your PowerPoint presentation, choose the Save command.

▶   From the File menu, choose Save (CTRL+S).

A dialog box doesn't appear, because the presentation already has a name. The current information in your presentation is saved with the same name.

One Step Further

You have learned to start Graph, create a graph using basic features, exit Graph, and edit a graph from PowerPoint. If you'd like to practice these and other basic skills in your practice presentation, try the following:

▶ From the Format menu, select the Color Palette, choose a scheme color in the left column by clicking it, and then click the Edit button. Customize your graph color by changing the amount of color, hue, saturation, and luminosity.

▶ Change your graph format using the Gallery menu.

▶ Design a graph in PowerPoint and then copy it to another presentation or application.

If you want to continue to the next lesson

1   From the File menu, choose Close (CTRL+F4).

2   If a dialog box appears asking if you want to save the changes to the presentation, click the No button. You do not need to save the changes you've made to the presentation since you printed it.

Choosing this command closes the active presentation; it does not exit PowerPoint. If no other presentations are open, the menu bar displays two available menus: File and Help.

If you want to quit PowerPoint for now

1   From the File menu, choose Exit.

2   If a dialog box is appears asking if you want to save changes to the presentation, click the No button.

Lesson Summary

To	Do this
Start Graph	On the Tool Palette click the Graph tool and drag to draw a box.
Change graph formats	From the Graph menu, choose Gallery.
Apply a different color	From the Format menu, choose Color Palette.
Change a graph color	From the Color Palette, click the Edit button.
Exit Graph	From the File menu, choose Exit and Return.

To	Do this
Update your presentation without leaving Graph	From the File menu, choose Update.
Edit your graph from PowerPoint	Double-click your graph.
Reposition your graph on a slide	Click and drag the graph object.

For more information on	See the *Microsoft PowerPoint Handbook*
Graphing in PowerPoint	Chapter 11, "Graphing"
Editing objects	Chapter 4, "Working with PowerPoint Objects"
PowerPoint color schemes	Chapter 6, "Working with Color Schemes"

Preview of the Next Lesson

In the next lesson, you'll learn to select, enter, edit, move, and delete data in a datasheet, import data from Microsoft Excel, and modify data in rows and columns. By the end of the lesson, you'll have produced another presentation for your quick-reference notebook.

Editing Graph Data

Graph data is composed of individual cells that form rows and columns which make up groups of related data points called a *data series.* The information in a data series represents one or more data markers on a graph. Editing data requires moving through a datasheet and working with individual cells and groups of cells.

In this lesson, you'll learn how to select individual cells and groups of cells for editing, move through a datasheet, move and delete a data series, import data from a Microsoft Excel spreadsheet, and modify a data series. At the end of the lesson, your presentation will consist of the following slides:

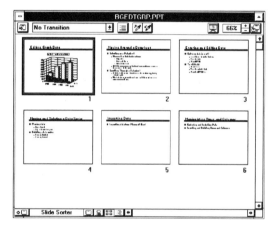

This lesson explains how to do the following:

- Select cells in a datasheet
- Scroll through a datasheet
- Enter data in a datasheet
- Edit data on a datasheet
- Move and delete data
- Import data from Microsoft Excel
- Modify a data series

Estimated lesson time: 25 minutes

Open a presentation

If you haven't already started PowerPoint, do so now. For instructions about starting PowerPoint, see "Getting Ready," earlier in this book.

1   From the File menu, choose Open (CTRL+O).

2   In the Directories box, be sure the PRACTICE directory is open. If it is not, select the drive where the Step by Step practice files are stored and open the appropriate directories to find the PRACTICE directory.

For information about   **3**   In the list of file names, choose LESSON09.PPT.
opening a sample
presentation, refer to   If you do not see LESSON09.PPT in the list of file names, check to be sure the
Lesson 2.   correct drive and directory are selected. If you need help, see "Getting Ready."

4   Click the OK button.

Your presentation opens to the following slide:

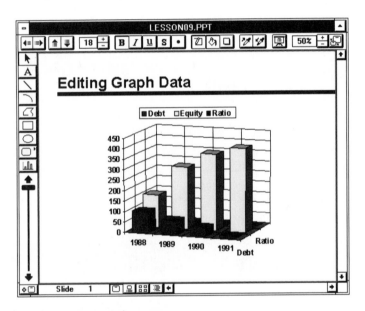

Save the presentation with a new name

Give the presentation a new name so the changes you make in this lesson will not overwrite the original presentation.

1   From the File menu, choose Save As.

2   In the File Name box, type y*our initials*edtgrp

For example, if your initials are B.G, type **bgedtgrp**

3   Click the OK button.

Preview the lesson

The presentation for this lesson contains reference information about editing Graph data. To preview the information in this lesson, click the Slide Show button on the Toolbar and view the on-screen presentation.

Slide Show

1 On the Toolbar, click the Slide Show button.

PowerPoint displays the first slide in the presentation.

2 Click to advance to the next slide.

3 Click once for each slide to advance through the rest of the presentation.

After the last slide in the presentation, PowerPoint returns to the current view.

Selecting Items in a Datasheet

On a datasheet, using the mouse or keyboard commands, you can select an individual cell, a range of cells or an entire row or column. When one cell is selected it is highlighted with a heavy border. When more than one cell is selected, the *active cell* is highlighted with a heavy border and all other selected cells are highlighted in black.To perform most tasks on the datasheet, you must select the cell or range of cells you want to work with.

Start Microsoft Graph

1 On the first slide, double-click the graph.

The Graph window appears.

2 From the Window menu, choose Datasheet.

The datasheet window moves in front of the chart window.

Tip To make any window the active window, click anywhere on that window.

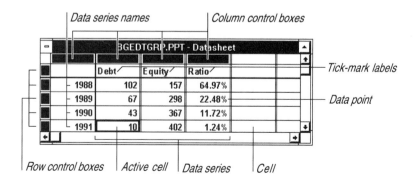

Scrolling Through a Datasheet

The data entered in the Graph datasheet plots on your Graph chart. As you enter data, the datasheet can become large, preventing you from seeing all the data at once. Graph allows you to scroll through the datasheet window to view different areas of the Datasheet window.

Use scroll bars, found on the right and bottom edges of the datasheet window to move around the datasheet. As you scroll through the datasheet, only the window view changes; an active cell or current selection is not affected by scrolling.

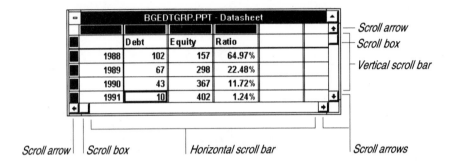

Scroll arrow · Scroll box · Horizontal scroll bar · Scroll arrows

Scroll arrow — Scroll box — Vertical scroll bar

Scroll in a datasheet

The following table explains how to scroll in a datasheet to view different cells:

To	Do this
Scroll one row or column at a time	Click a scroll arrow at either end of a scroll bar.
Scroll the datasheet one window up or down, left or right	Click on either side of the scroll box.
Scroll to a specific location	Drag the scroll box to the general location.

1 Click the scroll arrows to view sections of the datasheet.

2 Click and drag the scroll boxes to position the datasheet window back to the upper left corner of the datasheet.

3 Click the datasheet Maximize button.

The datasheet fills the Graph window.

		Debt	Equity	Ratio		
	1988	102	157	64.97%		
	1989	67	298	22.48%		
	1990	43	367	11.72%		
	1991	10	402	1.24%		

BGEDTGRP.PPT - Datasheet

Click here to maximize window

Select a cell

▶ Position the pointer over any cell and click.

A heavy border appears around the cell indicating it is selected.

Note To deselect a cell, a range, a row, a column, or a datasheet, click the pointer away from the selection.

Select a range

When two or more cells are selected, the first one selected is the active cell.

Select a range of cells by holding down the SHIFT key and clicking the cells you want to select.

1 Select the cell "1991."

2 SHIFT+click the cell "298."

A range of cells, 3 x 3, selects. You can also click and drag to select a range.

Your datasheet window should look similar to the following illustration:

Microsoft Graph - Graph in BGEDTGRP.PPT - Datasheet

File	Edit	DataSeries	Gallery	Chart	Format	Window	Help

		Debt	Equity	Ratio			
	1988	102	157	64.97%			
	1989	67	298	22.48%			
	1990	43	367	11.72%			
	1991	10	402	1.24%			

Select a row or column

Select a row or column by clicking on the row or column control box. Row and column control boxes are the black and gray boxes located along the left and top of the datasheet. If a control box is black, the data series is active and appears on the graph. If the control box is gray, the data series is inactive and doesn't appear on the graph.

1   Select the row control box for the year "1990."

	Debt	Equity	Ratio		
1988	102	157	64.97%		
1989	67	298	22.48%		
1990	43	367	11.72%		
1991	10	402	1.24%		

Microsoft Graph - Graph in BGEDTGRP.PPT - Datasheet

File   Edit   DataSeries   Gallery   Chart   Format   Window   Help

Click here to select an entire row

2   Select the column control box above the word "Equity."

The entire column selects.

Select the datasheet

1   From the Edit menu, choose Select All (CTRL+A).

The entire datasheet selects.

Tip   Click the box at the intersection of the row and column control boxes to select the entire datasheet.

---

2   Click any cell to deselect the datasheet.

Entering and Editing Data

In your datasheet, you'll enter data which will be used to plot data points and label data series on your graph.

Enter data in the datasheet

1 Select the empty cell below the year "1991."

2 Type **1992** and press ENTER.

Graph places your entry in the cell and activates the data series.

3 Press TAB to move to the next cell (the Debt column).

4 Type **28** and press ENTER.

Graph enters 28 in the datasheet and creates a new column for your graph.

Note The chart might be obscured by the datasheet, so you might not see the new column that is added to the chart. You can resize the Graph window by clicking and dragging the window edge.

---

5 Press TAB, then type **200** in the next cell and then press ENTER.

Your datasheet window should look similar to the following illustration:

Microsoft Graph - Graph in BGEDTGRP.PPT - Datasheet			
File Edit DataSeries Gallery Chart Format Window Help			
	Debt	Equity	Ratio
1988	102	157	64.97%
1989	67	298	22.48%
1990	43	367	11.72%
1991	10	402	1.24%
1992	28	200	

Edit data in the datasheet

1 Type **180** and press ENTER.

Graph replaces the number 200 with the new number.

Tip   Double-clicking a cell displays a Cell Data dialog box in which you can change cell information.

Moving and Deleting a Data Series

In Graph, you can move and reposition information within the same datasheet to facilitate editing tasks. Graph allows you to copy information to other places in the datasheet. You can also cut information from your datasheet to move it elsewhere.

Copy data in the datasheet

1   Select the column control box above the word "Debt."

2   From the Edit menu, choose Copy (CTRL+C).

3   Select the empty cell to the right of the word "Ratio."

4   From the Edit menu, choose Paste (CTRL+V).

Graph duplicates the Debt column in a new column next to the Ratio column.

Move data within the datasheet

1   Select the row control box for the year 1989.

2   From the Edit menu, choose Cut (CTRL+X).

The row control box becomes inactive, and the data in the row deletes.

Note   Graph, like PowerPoint, uses the Clipboard to store information that you cut or copy from a datasheet until you paste the information to its new location.

---

3   Select the empty cell below the year "1992."

4   From the Edit menu, choose Paste.

The 1989 row is now directly below the 1992 row.

Clear data from the datasheet

1   SHIFT+click the Control box for the 1992 row.

Graph selects both the 1989 and the 1992 rows.

TROUBLESHOOTING: **If only the row 1992 is selected**   The row for 1989 was deselected before selecting the 1992 row. SHIFT+click the Control box for the 1989 row.

Your datasheet window should look similar to the following illustration:

Microsoft Graph - Graph in BGEDTGRP.PPT - Datasheet							
File	Edit	DataSeries	Gallery	Chart	Format	Window	Help
		Debt	Equity	Ratio	Debt		
	1988	102	157	64.97%	102		
	1990	43	367	11.72%	43		
	1991	10	402	1.24%	10		
	1992	28	180		28		
	1989	67	298	22.48%	67		

2 From the Edit menu, choose Clear.

The Clear dialog box appears.

3 Click the Clear Both option button.

*Click here to clear
both data and formats
from selected cells*

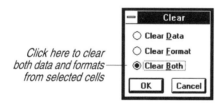

4 Click the OK button.

The two bottom rows selected in your datasheet clear.

TROUBLESHOOTING: **If you accidentally clear (delete) the correct data** Immediately select Undo from the Graph Edit menu. The data cleared from your datasheet will be recovered and returned to the datasheet.

Importing Data

In addition to allowing you to type your own data into the datasheet, Graph allows you to directly import information from Microsoft Excel. You can also copy and paste a specified range of data or a complete spreadsheet into Graph.

Import data from Microsoft Excel

1 Select the cell to the left of the word "Debt."

2 From the File menu, choose Import Data.

3 In the Files box click the down scroll arrow and select SHEET09.XLS.

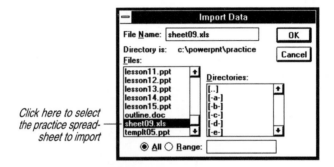

Click here to select the practice spreadsheet to import

4 Click the OK button.

A Microsoft Graph dialog box appears.

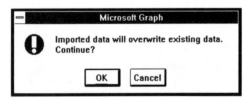

5 Click the OK button.

Your datasheet and chart update with the data from your Microsoft Excel spreadsheet and overwrite the existing datasheet.

Your datasheet window should look similar to the following illustration:

Microsoft Graph - Graph in BGEDTGRP.PPT - Datasheet				
File Edit DataSeries Gallery Chart Format Window Help				
	March	April	May	3-Month Total
Widgets	412	522	653	1587
Sprockets	400	390	460	1250
Cogs	240	350	330	920
Mallets	375	495	803	1673

Modifying a Data Series

After entering data on your datasheet, you might want to modify it to produce a more effective graph. You can exclude and include data by rows and columns, changing the effect of your graph without changing the datasheet information. You can also insert and delete rows and columns to accommodate the information in your datasheet.

Exclude and include data

1   Click the datasheet window Restore button.

The datasheet window minimizes.

Click here to minimize datasheet window

Microsoft Graph - Graph in BGEDTGRP.PPT - Datasheet				
File Edit DataSeries Gallery Chart Format Window Help				
	March	April	May	3-Month Total
Widgets	412	522	653	1587
Sprockets	400	390	460	1250

2 Click the Graph window Maximize button.

The Graph window showing the datasheet and chart windows fills the screen.

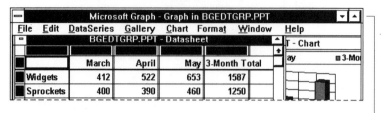

Click here to maximize Graph window

3 Move the datasheet and chart windows so you can see them both by clicking and dragging their title bars.

Your Graph window should look similar to the following illustration:

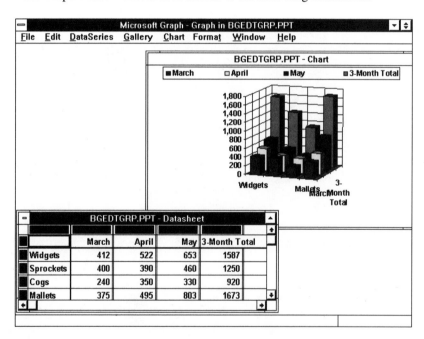

4 Select the column control box above "3-Month Total."

5 From the Data Series menu, choose Exclude Row/Col.

Graph dims the column heading for "3-Month Total," indicating the column has been excluded from the datasheet. The data from this column has also been excluded from the graph.

Your datasheet window should look similar to the following illustration:

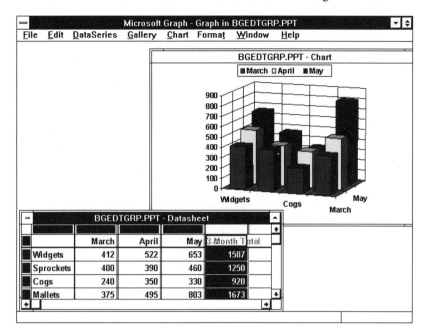

Note An excluded column or row remains excluded until you include the data, import information over the excluded data, or type over the excluded data.

6 Select the "3-Month Total" column control box.

7 From the Data Series menu, choose Include Row/Col.

The 3-Month Total column returns to your datasheet.

Insert columns and rows

Insert a new column to the left of a selected column.

1 Select the column control box above "March."

2 From the Edit menu, choose Insert Row/Col (CTRL++).

Graph inserts a new column to the left of the March column.

Your datasheet window should look similar to the following illustration:

3 From the Edit menu, choose Delete Row/Col (CTRL+ -).

The column entered in step 2 disappears.

4 Select the row control box next to the word "Sprockets."

5 From the Edit menu, choose Insert Row/Col.

Graph places a new row above the Sprockets row in the datasheet.

6 From the Edit menu, choose Delete Row/Col.

7 From the File menu choose Exit and Return.

8 Click the No button in the Update Graph Dialog box.

Print the quick-reference notebook presentation

For information on printing a presentation, refer to Lesson 13.

1 From the File menu, choose Print (CTRL+P).

The Print dialog box appears.

2 Click the down arrow next to the Print box.

3 Click Handouts (2 slides per page) from the drop-down list.

4 Click the OK button.

A dialog box appears to give your printing status.

Save the Presentation

▶ From the File menu, choose Save (CTRL+S).

A dialog box doesn't appear, because the presentation already has a name. The current information in your presentation is saved with the same name.

One Step Further

You have learned to select and scroll on a datasheet, edit and move data in Graph, import data from a Microsoft Excel chart, and modify a data series. If you'd like to practice these and other basic skills in your practice presentation, try the following:

▶ Exclude the 3-Month Total column and from the Gallery select 3-D Pie.

▶ Add additional data series and data points.

▶ Reposition the location of one or more data series and notice the affect on the graph.

▶ If you have a copy of Microsoft Excel, import a spreadsheet and create a chart with the data.

If you want to continue to the next lesson

1 From the File menu, choose Close (CTRL+F4).

2 If a dialog box appears asking if you want to save the changes to the presentation, click the No button. You do not need to save the changes you made to the presentation after you printed it.

Choosing this command closes the active presentation; it does not exit PowerPoint. If no other presentations are open, the menu bar displays two available menus: File and Help.

If you want to quit PowerPoint for now

1 From the File menu, choose Exit.

2 If a dialog box appears asking if you want to save changes to the presentation, click the No button.

Lesson Summary

To	Do this
Select a cell in Graph	Move your pointer to the cell and click.
Select a cell range	SHIFT+click the cells you want to select or click and drag across a group of cells.
Select a row or column	Move the pointer to the row or column control box and click.
Select all the cells in the datasheet	Move your pointer to the intersecting cell between the row and column headings, or from the Edit menu choose Select All.
Scroll through a datasheet	Click the datasheet scroll bars.
Enter data	Click the cell, type your information, and press the ENTER key.
Edit data	Click the cell and type the new information.
Move data	To copy, cut, or clear data, select the data and use the cut or copy command, then the paste command.
Import data	Select any cell in the datasheet. From the Edit menu, choose Import Data.
Exclude/Include data	Select the row or column. From the Data Series menu, choose Exclude Row/Col or Include Row/Col.
Insert/Delete rows or columns	Select the row or column you want to insert or delete. From the Edit menu, choose Insert Row/Col or Delete Row/Col.

For more information on	See the *Microsoft PowerPoint Handbook*
Editing Graph Data	Chapter 11, "Graphing"

Preview of the Next Lesson

In the next lesson, you'll learn to change a graph format, add titles and data labels, change the axis scale, and work with the legend. By the end of the lesson, you'll have produced another presentation for your quick-reference notebook.

Formatting a Graph

In PowerPoint Graph you can change the appearance of your graph at any time. Simply double-click the graph you would like to change. You can control the way your graph looks by choosing various features such as font styles, arrows, and legends.

In this lesson, you'll learn how to format a graph using a 3-D view, work with a legend, format data cells, apply and format arrows, work with axes, and format axis scales. At the end of the lesson, your presentation will consist of the following slides:

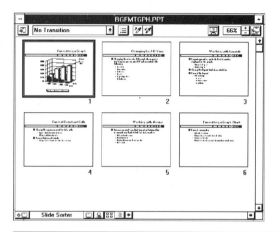

This lesson explains how to do the following:

- Format a 3-D graph
- Format datasheet cells
- Change tick-mark formats
- Format a legend
- Work with arrows
- Format axes in your graph

Estimated lesson time: 35 minutes

Open a presentation

If you haven't already started PowerPoint, do so now. For instructions about starting PowerPoint, see "Getting Ready," earlier in this book.

1   From the File menu, choose Open (CTRL+O).

2   In the Directories box, be sure the PRACTICE directory is open. If it is not, select the drive where the Step by Step practice files are stored and open the appropriate directories to find the PRACTICE directory.

For information about opening a sample presentation, refer to Lesson 2.

3   In the list of file names, click LESSON10.PPT.

If you do not see LESSON10.PPT in the list of file names, check to be sure the correct drive and directory are selected. If you need help, see "Getting Ready."

4   Click the OK button.

Your presentation opens to the following slide:

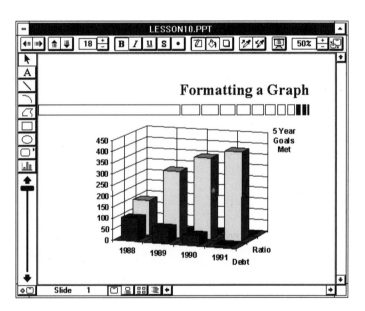

Save the presentation with a new name

Give the presentation a new name so the changes you make in this lesson will not overwrite the original document.

1   From the File menu, choose Save As.

2   In the File Name box, type *your initials***fmtgph**

For example, if your initials are B.G., type **bgfmtgph**

3   Click the OK button.

Preview the lesson

The presentation for this lesson contains reference information about formatting a graph. To preview the information in this lesson, click the Slide Show button on the Toolbar and view the on-screen presentation.

Slide Show

1   On the Toolbar, click the Slide Show button.

PowerPoint displays the first slide in the presentation.

2   Click to advance to the next slide.

3   Click once for each slide to advance through the rest of the presentation.

After the last slide in the presentation, PowerPoint returns to the current view.

Formatting a 3-D Graph

You can control the position and perspective of 3-D graphs.

1   Double-click the graph on slide 1.

The graph window appears.

Note   If the chart is not in full view, click the title bar and drag it closer to the center of the Graph window.

Graph Datasheet window (behind chart)

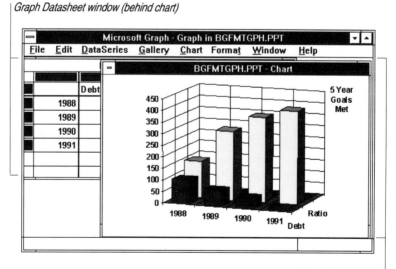

Graph Chart window

2   From the Format menu, choose 3-D View.

The Format 3-D View dialog box appears.

3   Click the up Elevation arrow until the Elevation box shows 50.

The sample graph in the center of the dialog box shows the results of format changes as they are made in the dialog box.

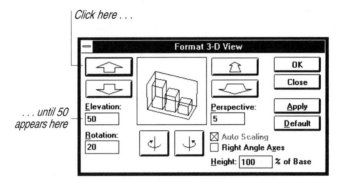

4   Click the left Rotation button until the Rotation box shows 70.

The dialog box should look similar to the following illustration:

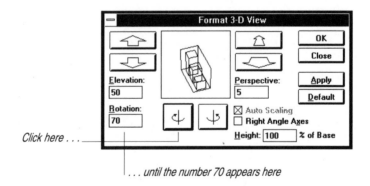

5   Click the OK button.

Your graph should look similar to the following illustration:

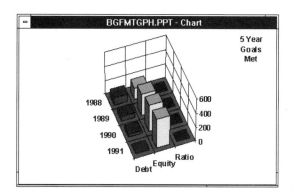

For information on data series names and other datasheet components, refer to Lesson 9.

The elevation, rotation, and data series names have changed to match the changes you made in the 3-D View dialog box.

The Format 3-D View dialog box allows you to change six options:

- **Elevation**   The elevation controls the height at which you view your graph. All 3-D graphs, except for 3-D pie graphs, can range from -90 degrees to +90 degrees.

- **Rotation**   This option controls the rotation of the plot area around the z–axis (vertical axis). You can rotate your graph from 0 degrees to 360 degrees.

- **Perspective**   Provides a distance perspective. More perspective makes data markers at the back of the graph grow smaller than the markers in the front of the graph.

- **Right Angle Axes**   Controls the orientation of the axes. Select the check box to show axes at right angles to each other. Clearing the check box shows the axes in perspective.

- **Auto Scaling**   Use this option when changing from a 2-D graph to a 3-D graph. 3-D graphs sometimes draw smaller.

- **Height**   Controls the height of the z-axis and walls relative to the length of the x-axis, or width of the base of the graph. The height is measured based on a percentage of the x-axis length.

Practice for a moment

- From the Format 3-D View dialog box, change the elevation to -25 and the rotation to 40. Click the OK button.

- Change the elevation, rotation, and perspective options as desired and look at the results on your graph.

- When you are finished, set the elevation to 10, the rotation to 20, the perspective to 5, and click the OK button.

Working with Legends

Legends represent data series markers in a graph using color or patterns. Each color or pattern corresponds to a specific data series name in the graph. Graph legends can be positioned automatically or manually. Legends can be formatted with different colors, font styles, and patterns. Data series names and category names supply text for the legend.

Add a legend

▶ From the Chart menu, choose Add Legend.

Graph places the legend in its default position on the right side of the plot area and resizes the plot to accommodate the legend.

Change your legend's appearance

1   From the Format menu, select Patterns.

The Area Patterns dialog box appears.

2   Click the down arrows in the Area Patterns dialog box and view the option lists.

3   In the Border box, click the Shadow check box.

Graph puts a shadow behind the legend. The Area Patterns dialog box should look similar to the following illustration:

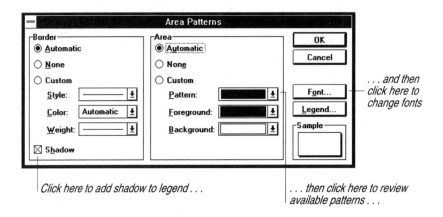

... and then click here to change fonts

Click here to add shadow to legend . . .

. . . then click here to review available patterns . . .

Tip   To reset the border or area attributes to the default settings, click the Automatic check box or click the Cancel button.

---

4   Click the Font button.

The Chart Fonts dialog box appears.

5   In the Fonts box, select Book Antiqua.

6 In the Size box, select 16.

The dialog box should look similar to the following:

Click here to select font

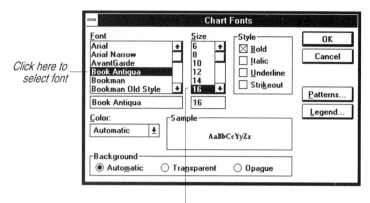

Click here to select font size

7 Click the Legend button.

The Legend dialog box appears.

8 In the Type box, click the Top option button.

Click here to move legend to top

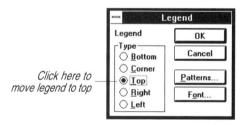

9 Click the OK button.

Graph applies all three changes (shadow, font and position) to your legend as shown in the following illustration:

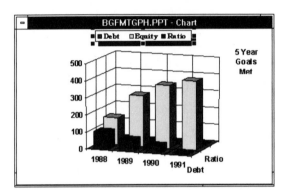

Move your legend manually

1 Click and drag the legend until it touches the left side of the chart.

Graph repositions the graph plot and all other items to accommodate the new position of the legend as shown in the following illustration:

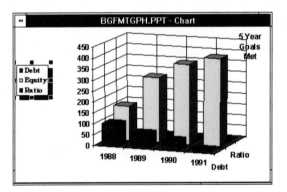

TROUBLESHOOTING: **If the legend overlays part of the chart**   Drag the legend further toward the left edge of the chart. A vertical line appears on the left edge of the chart indicating the chart will be resized and repositioned to accommodate the legend.

2 From the Format menu, choose Legend.

3 In the Type box, click the Bottom option button.

4 Click the OK button.

Formatting Datasheet Cells

You can change the appearance of datasheet cells by applying different font characteristics, and colors.

Note Changing the font characteristics in your datasheet affects all of the datasheet cells but not the chart text.

Change the font style

1 Click anywhere on the datasheet to make it the active window.

2 From the Format menu, choose Font.

The Datasheet Font dialog box appears.

3 In the Font box, select Arial Narrow.

4 Click the OK button.

All of the data in your datasheet changes to the font Arial Narrow.

Change number formatting

1 Select the word "Debt" in your datasheet.

2 SHIFT+click cell "402."

Your datasheet window should look similar to the following illustration:

For information on number formats, refer to your PowerPoint Handbook, Chapter 11.

3 From the Format menu, choose Number

The Number dialog box appears.

4 In the Number Format scroll box, select the numeric format, "$#,##0;($#,##0)."

Click here to select numeric format

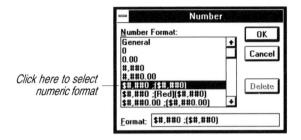

5 Click the OK button

Graph formats the Debt and Equity columns with dollar signs.

Change tick-mark labels

▶ Click anywhere on the chart window to make it the active window.

Graph formats the tick-marks on the vertical axis with dollar signs as shown in the following illustration:

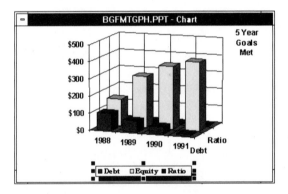

Tip   The numeric format of the vertical axis follows the format of the first data cell in the datasheet.

Formatting Arrows

Graph uses arrows to call out important information or connect unattached text to a specific data marker on the graph plot. Graph arrows are objects and can be modified like any other PowerPoint object.

Add an arrow

1   From the Chart menu, choose Add Arrow.

An arrow appears on the chart with resize handles on both ends.

2   Move your pointer to the edit handle at the base of the arrow (end of the arrow without the point).

The pointer, when placed over the edit handle, changes to the cross hairs cursor, indicating that end of the arrow can be moved.

3   Click and drag the base of the arrow to a point near the text "5 Year Goals Met."

4   Click and drag the arrowhead to a point near the top of the "1989 Equity" column.

5   Click in the blank area of the plot to deselect the arrow.

Your graph should look similar to the following illustration:

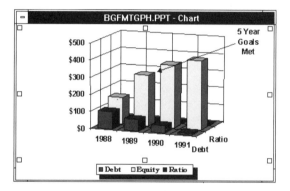

Note   Clicking off the arrow deselects the arrow and simultaneously selects another item in the chart.

Change an arrow

When an arrow is added to a graph, it is selected for editing purposes. Each time you format the arrow later, you must select it by clicking it or using the UP ARROW key or the DOWN ARROW key.

1   Select the arrow.

The resize handles return, indicating the arrow can be edited.

2   From the Format menu, choose Patterns.

The Line Patterns dialog box appears.

Note   The available options in the Patterns dialog box change depending on the item selected in your graph.

3 Click the down arrow in the color box.

4 Select any color.

5 Click the OK button.

Graph changes the arrow to the color you selected in the Line Patterns dialog box.

Formatting a Graph Chart

Axes are the scales data plots on in a graph. Axes can format independently to achieve desired effects. Two dimensional (2-D) graphs have two axes, a y-axis and an x-axis. The x-axis plots horizontally, and the y-axis plots vertically.

Three dimensional (3-D) graphs have three axes, an x-axis (category axis), y-axis (series axis), and a z-axis (value axis).

Format axes

1 From the Chart menu, choose Axes.

The 3-D Axes dialog box appears.

2 In the Main Chart box, click the Value (Z) Axis check box.

Click here to clear z-axis labels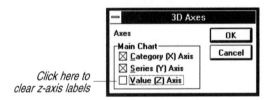

3 Click the OK button.

The z-axis value numbers clear from the graph.

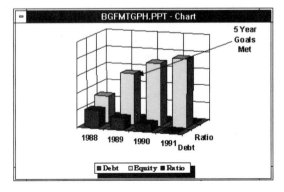

4 From the Chart menu, choose Axes.

5 In the Main Chart box, click the Value (Z) Axis check box.

6 Click the OK button.

The z-axis numbers return to your graph.

Format axis scales and tick-mark labels

Graph formats axis scales with different line and tick-mark styles, text orientations, font characteristics, and scale sizes.

1 Select the x-axis. (The horizontal axis.)

Edit handles appear on both ends of the axis.

Tip Double-clicking any item in the graph chart brings up an editing dialog box. For example, to open the editing dialog box for a gridline, move your pointer to the desired gridline and double-click. The Line Patterns dialog box appears.

---

2 From the Format menu, choose Patterns.

The Axis Patterns dialog box appears. Customize the axis style, color, and weight. and change how the tick-marks look in the Patterns dialog box.

3 In the Axis box, click the Weight down arrow.

A drop-down list appears.

4 Select the fourth line style in the drop-down list.

The new line style appears in the Weight box and in the Sample box.

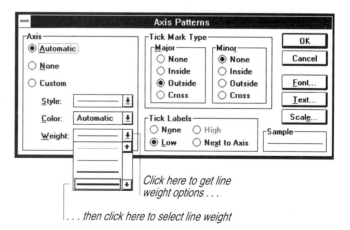

Click here to get line weight options . . .

. . . then click here to select line weight

5 Click the Font button.

6 In the Font box, click the down scroll arrow and select Times New Roman.

7 Click the Text button.

The Axis Text dialog box appears.

8 In the Orientation box, select the Text box just below the word "Automatic."

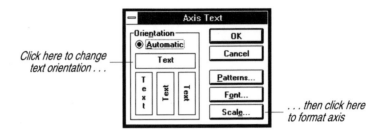

Click here to change text orientation . . .

. . . then click here to format axis

9 Click the Scale button.

The Format Axis Scale dialog box appears.

10 In the Between Tick Marks box, double-click the number 1.

11 Type **2**

The dialog box should look similar to the following illustration:

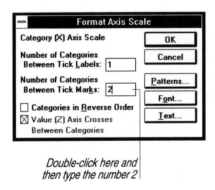

Double-click here and then type the number 2

12 Click the OK button.

Graph makes all your changes. The x-axis line is heavier, the tick-mark labels are in Times New Roman, and there is one tick-mark for every two categories, as seen in the following illustration:

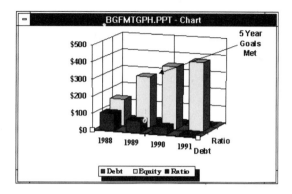

Exit Graph

1   From the Graph File menu, choose Exit and Return to BGFMTGPH.PPT.

A dialog box appears, asking if you want to save the changes made to your graph.

2   Click the Yes button.

Print the quick-reference notebook presentation

For information on printing a presentation, refer to Lesson 13.

1   From the File menu, choose Print (CTRL+P).

The Print dialog box appears.

2   Click the down arrow next to the Print box.

3   Select Handouts (2 slides per page) from the drop-down list.

4   Click the OK button.

A dialog box appears, to give your printing status.

Save the Presentation

To save your PowerPoint presentation, choose the Save command.

▶   From the File menu, choose Save (CTRL+S).

A dialog box doesn't appear, because the presentation already has a name. The current information in your presentation is saved with the same name.

One Step Further

You have learned to change the format of a 3-D graph, format a legend, change cell formatting, add and move arrows, and format axes scales. If you'd like to practice these and other basic skills in your practice presentation, try the following:

▶ Change the Gallery setting to other 3-D graphs and format the 3-D view.

▶ Apply different borders, patterns, and characteristics to your legend.

▶ Format your datasheet cells with different numbers.

▶ Add arrows to your graph and change the line pattern and style using the Patterns from the Format menu.

▶ Change the format of your axes using the Scale command from the Format menu.

If you want to continue to the next lesson

1   From the File menu, choose Close (CTRL+F4).

2   If a dialog box appears asking if you want to save changes to the presentation, click the No button. You do not need to save the changes you made to the presentation after you printed it.

Choosing this command closes the active presentation; it does not exit PowerPoint. If no other presentations are open, the menu bar displays two available menus: File and Help.

If you want to quit PowerPoint for now

1   From the File menu, choose Exit.

2   If a dialog box appears asking if you want to save changes to the presentation, click the No button.

Lesson Summary

To	Do this
Open an existing graph	Double-click on the graph.
Change the 3-D format of your graph	From the Format menu, choose 3-D View.
Edit a legend	Select the legend using your mouse or an UP ARROW key or DOWN ARROW key.
Add or delete a legend	From the Chart menu, Choose Add/Delete Legend.
Change legend characteristics	From the Format menu, choose Patterns.
Move a legend	Click and drag the legend for manual placement or choose Legend from the Format menu to place the legend.
Change cell numeric values	Select the cell(s) and choose Number from the Format menu.
Change datasheet font styles	From the Format menu, choose Font.
Change Tick–Mark labels	Select the first data cell (usually row 2, column 2) and choose Number from the Format menu.
Add/Delete an arrow	From the Chart menu, choose Add/Delete Arrow.
Select an arrow	Select the arrow or press the UP ARROW key or DOWN ARROW key.
Add/Delete axes	From the Chart menu, choose Axes.

For more information on	See the *Microsoft PowerPoint Handbook*
Formatting a Graph	Chapter 11, "Graphing"

Preview of the Next Lesson

In the next lesson, you'll learn how to copy and paste clip art, insert, recolor, and crop pictures and rescale objects. At the end of the lesson, you'll have another presentation for your quick-reference notebook.

5 Inserting and Linking Information

Inserting Information into PowerPoint

You can bring information into PowerPoint in several ways. The most straightforward way is to copy and paste the information. You can copy and paste text, objects, and slides within a presentation, among presentations, and to other Windows-based applications. PowerPoint uses the Windows Clipboard,which stores the copied information, to paste information into PowerPoint presentations. Another way to bring information into PowerPoint is to use the Insert command, which allows you to insert an entire object, picture, or outline.

In this lesson, you'll learn how to copy and paste clip art to a slide, use a timesaver diagram, scale an object, and insert, crop, and recolor a picture. At the end of the lesson, your presentation will consist of the following slides:

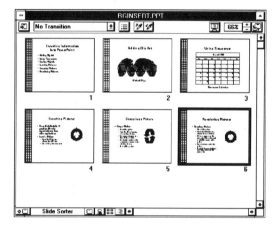

This lesson explains how to do the following:

- Add clip art to a slide
- Use a timesaver diagram
- Scale an object
- Insert a picture
- Crop a picture
- Recolor a picture

Estimated lesson time: 20 minutes

Open a presentation

If you haven't already started PowerPoint, do so now. For instructions about starting PowerPoint, see "Getting Ready," earlier in this book.

1 From the File menu, choose Open (CTRL+O).

2 In the Directories box, be sure the PRACTICE directory is open. If it is not, select the drive where the Step by Step practice files are stored and open the appropriate directories to find the PRACTICE directory.

For information about opening a sample presentation, refer to Lesson 2.

3 In the list of file names, click LESSON11.PPT.

If you do not see LESSON11.PPT in the list of file names, check to be sure the correct drive and directory are selected. If you need help, see "Getting Ready."

4 Click the OK button.

Your presentation opens to the following slide:

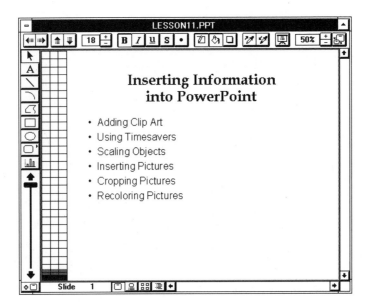

Save the presentation with a new name

Give the presentation a new name so the changes you make in this lesson will not overwrite the original presentation.

1 From the File menu, choose Save As.

2 In the File Name box, type *your initials***insert**

For example, if your initials are B. G., type **bginsert**

3 Click the OK button.

Preview the lesson

The presentation for this lesson contains reference information about inserting information into PowerPoint. To preview the information in this lesson, click the Slide Show button on the Toolbar and view the on-screen presentation.

Slide Show

1   On the Toolbar, click the Slide Show button.

PowerPoint displays the first slide in the presentation.

2   Click to advance to the next slide.

3   Click once for each slide to advance through the rest of the presentation.

After the last slide in the presentation, PowerPoint returns to the current view.

Change to the next slide

▶   Click the down arrow on the Slide Changer to advance to slide 2.

Adding Clip Art

PowerPoint comes with over 500 professionally designed pieces of clip art to use in your presentation to help you get your message across. The Open Clip Art command makes it easy to find the clip art category that best meets your needs.

Paste clip art to a slide

1   From the File menu, choose Open Clip Art.

The Open Clip Art dialog box appears with a list of clip art files.

2   In the list of file names, click INTLMAPS.PPT.

If you do not see INTLMAPS.PPT in the list of file names, check to be sure the correct drive and directory are selected. If you need help, see "Getting Ready."

3   Click the OK button.

4   Double-click the slide icon for slide 8.

Slide 8 appears with a World Map.

5   Select the World Map object.

6   From the Edit menu, choose Copy (CTRL+C).

The World Map object copies to the Windows Clipboard.

7   From the File menu, choose Close (CTRL+F4).

The INTLMAPS.PPT clip art file closes.

8   From the Edit menu, choose Paste (CTRL+V).

The World Map object pastes on slide 2.

Your presentation window should look similar to the following illustration:

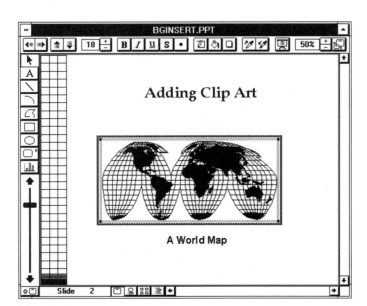

Change to the next slide

▶ Click the down arrow on the Slide Changer to advance to slide 3.

Using Timesavers

PowerPoint timesavers are a collection of six presentations with common presentation diagrams you can use in your presentation to save time. The collection of diagrams includes calendars, flowcharts, graphs, organizational charts, tables, and timelines.

Use a timesaver diagram

1 From the File menu, choose Open.

2 In the Directories box, double-click the POWERPNT directory.

3 In the Directories box, double-click the TIMESAVR directory.

4 In the File Names box, select CALENDAR.PPT.

   If you do not see CALENDAR.PPT in the list of file names, check to be sure the correct drive and directory are selected. If you need help, see "Getting Ready."

The Open dialog box should look similar to the following illustration:

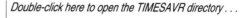

Double-click here to open the TIMESAVR directory . . .

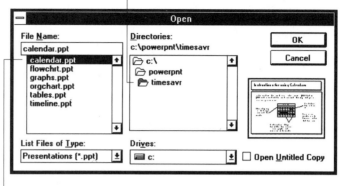

. . . then click here to select the CALENDAR.PPT presentation

5   Click the OK button.

The CALENDAR.PPT file opens up in Outline view.

6   Double-click the slide icon for slide 3.

Slide 3 appears, displaying August 1992 as shown in the following illustration:

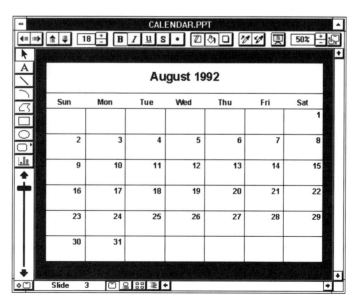

7   Select the calendar object.

8   From the Edit menu, choose Copy.

The August 1992 calendar object copies to the Windows Clipboard.

9   From the File menu, choose Close.

The CALENDER.PPT file closes.

10   From the Edit menu, choose Paste.

The calendar object pastes on slide 3.

Note   The calendar is too large to fit properly on the slide. In the next section you'll resize the calendar to fit on your slide.

You can edit the calendar by double-clicking the object, which converts the picture to PowerPoint objects. Use the Ungroup command to edit individual objects and then the Regroup command to reassemble the objects.

Scaling Objects

Scaling is resizing an entire object by a percentage. With the Scale command you can resize an object numerically instead of by dragging. An object can be scaled relative to the original picture size if an X appears in the check box in the Scale dialog box.

Scale an object

1   Select the calendar object if it is not currently selected.

2   From the Object menu, choose Scale.

The Scale dialog box appears.

3   In the Scale To box, type **70**

The scale size applies to the object right after you type so you can see how the object will look before leaving the dialog box.

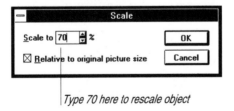

Type 70 here to rescale object

4   Click the OK button.

5   Click and drag the calendar object to center it under the slide title.

Your presentation window should look similar to the following illustration:

Tip   PowerPoint remembers the original size of a picture or text object. If you accidently change the size of an object, set the scale back to 100% relative to its original size.

Change to the next slide

▶ Click the down arrow on the Slide Changer to advance to slide 4.

Inserting a Picture

If you have created graphics in other applications, you can insert them into PowerPoint with the Insert Picture command. PowerPoint can insert eleven different graphic formats. A list can be found in Appendix A, "Installing Microsoft PowerPoint."

Insert a picture

1 From the Edit menu, choose Insert, and then choose Picture.

The Insert Picture dialog box appears. (This dialog box functions just like the Open dialog box.)

2 In the Directories box, double-click the PRACTICE directory.

3   In the list of file names, click LOGO1.TIF.

If you do not see LOGO1.TIF in the list of file names, check to be sure the correct drive and directory are selected. If you need help, see "Getting Ready."

4   Click the OK button.

An arrow logo pastes on slide 4.

5   Click and drag the logo to the right of the body text.

Your presentation window should look similar to the following illustration:

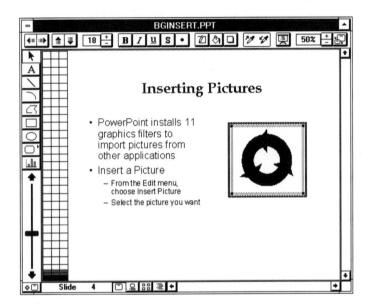

Change to the next slide

▶   Click the down arrow on the Slide Changer to advance to slide 5.

Cropping a Picture

Sometimes you need only a portion of a picture in your presentation. With the Crop Picture command, you can cover portions of a picture so you don't see all of it on the screen. The picture is not altered, just covered up.

Crop a picture

1   Select the Curved Arrows object.

Cropping Tool

2   From the Object menu, choose Crop Picture.

The pointer changes to the Cropping tool.

3   Position the center of the Cropping tool over the bottom right resize handle.

4   Click and drag to the left to crop the right curved arrow.

A dotted outline displays when cropping to show you the cropped area when you release the mouse button. The Cropping tool also changes to indicate you're cropping.

Your presentation window should look similar to the following illustration:

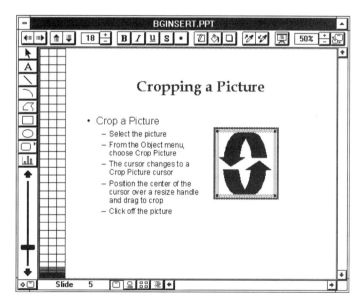

5   Click anywhere to deactivate the Cropping tool.

The Cropping tool changes to the pointer.

Change to the next slide

▶   Click the down arrow on the Slide Changer to advance to slide 6.

Recoloring a Picture

Pictures can be recolored to follow a new color scheme. The Recolor Picture command displays a dialog box with a preview of the picture and a list of all the colors in the picture. Each color in the list can be individually changed.

Recolor a picture

1   Select the Circular Three Arrows object.

2   From the Object menu, choose Recolor Picture.

   The Recolor dialog box appears.

3   Click the drop-down arrow next to GY8.

   A color menu appears.

4   Select the color B.

   GY8 changes to B. An **X** appears in the Change check box indicating you changed a color.

5   Click the drop-down arrow next to GY4 and select the green color between the color B and the color R.

6   Click the drop-down arrow next to GY6 and select the color R.

7   Click the Preview button to see your changes.

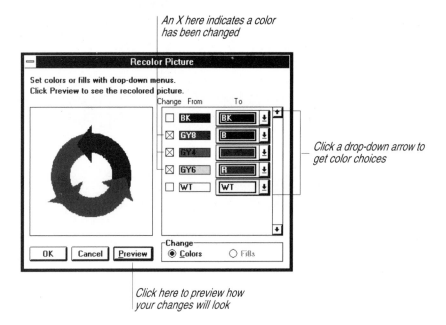

An X here indicates a color has been changed

Click a drop-down arrow to get color choices

Click here to preview how your changes will look

8   Click the OK button.

PowerPoint recolors the arrow object.

Print the quick-reference notebook presentation

For information on printing a presentation, refer to Lesson 13.

1   From the File menu, choose Print (CTRL+P).

The Print dialog box appears.

2   Click the down arrow next to the Print box.

3   Click Handouts (2 slides per page) from the drop-down list.

4   Click the OK button.

A dialog box appears to give your printing status.

Save the Presentation

▶   From the File menu, choose Save (CTRL+S).

A dialog box doesn't appear, because the presentation already has a name. The current information in your presentation is saved with the same name.

One Step Further

You have learned how to add clip art and timesavers to your presentation, scale objects, and insert, crop, and recolor pictures. If you'd like to practice these and other basic skills in your practice presentation, try the following:

1   Copy and paste clip art or timesaver objects into your presentation.

2   Scale the objects.

3   Crop and recolor the objects.

If you want to continue to the next lesson

1   From the File menu, choose Close.

2   If a dialog box appears asking if you want to save the changes to your presentation, click the No button. You do not need to save the changes you made to the presentation after you printed it.

Choosing this command closes the active presentation; it does not exit PowerPoint. If no other presentations are open, the menu bar displays two available menus: File and Help.

If you want to quit PowerPoint for now

1   From the File menu, choose Exit.

2   If a dialog box appears asking if you want to save changes to the presentation, click the No button.

Lesson Summary

To	Do this
Add clip art	From the File menu, choose Open Clip Art. Open a file and select a piece of clip art. From the Edit menu, choose Copy. Switch to where you want the clip art. From the Edit menu, choose Paste.
Use a timesaver diagram	From the File menu, choose Open. Open a timesaver file and select a diagram. From the Edit menu, choose Copy. Switch to where you want the diagram. From the Edit menu, choose Paste.
Scale an object	Select the object. From the Object menu, choose Scale. Type a percentage.
Insert a picture	From the Edit menu, choose Insert, and then choose Picture. Select a file.
Crop a picture	From the Object menu, choose Crop Picture. Click and drag a resize handle.
Recolor a picture	From the Object menu, choose Recolor Picture. Click the drop-down arrow for each color and select a new one from the list. Click the Preview button to view your changes. Click the OK button.

For more information on	See the *Microsoft PowerPoint Handbook*
Inserting Information into PowerPoint	Chapter 12, "Using PowerPoint with Other Applications"
Clip Art	Appendix B, "Clip Art"

Preview of the Next Lesson

In the next lesson, you'll create a document and picture link, update changes to linked objects, cancel a link, and embed an object to a PowerPoint slide. By the end of the lesson, you'll have produced another presentation for your quick-reference notebook.

Linking Information with Other Applications

You can copy, link, or embed information from other applications into PowerPoint. To make updating easier, link or embed a document to a PowerPoint slide instead of just copying the document. If you link a document, updates to that document automatically appear. This ensures that your presentation always shows the latest information. If you want to edit a document quickly, embed the document. With an embedded document, you just double-click the document to open it for editing. When you close the document in the embedded application, any changes you make are reflected in your PowerPoint presentation.

In this lesson, you'll learn how to create a link to a document and picture, update, change, and cancel a link, and embed an object to a PowerPoint slide. At the end of the lesson, your presentation will consist of the following slides:

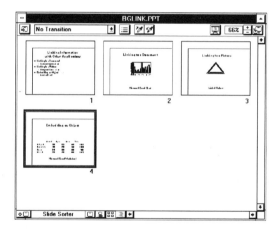

This lesson explains how to do the following:

- Link a document to a slide

- Edit a linked document

- Link a picture to a slide

- Change and cancel a link

- Embed an object to a slide

Estimated lesson time: 20 minutes

Open a presentation

If you haven't already started PowerPoint, do so now. For instructions about starting PowerPoint, see "Getting Ready," earlier in this book.

1 From the File menu, choose Open (CTRL+O).

2 In the Directories box, be sure the PRACTICE directory is open. If it is not, select the drive where the Step by Step practice files are stored and open the appropriate directories to find the PRACTICE directory.

For information about opening a sample presentation, refer to Lesson 2.

3 In the list of file names, click LESSON12.PPT.

If you do not see LESSON12.PPT in the list of file names, check to be sure the correct drive and directory are selected. If you need help, see "Getting Ready."

4 Click the OK button.

Your presentation opens to the following slide:

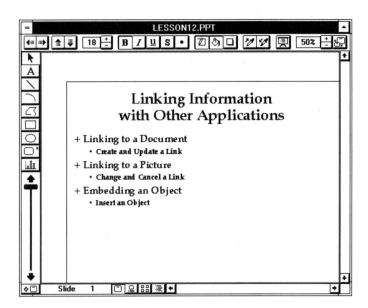

Save the presentation with a new name

Give the presentation a new name so the changes you make in this lesson will not overwrite the original presentation.

1 From the File menu, choose Save As.

2 In the File Name box, type *your initials***link**

For example, if your initials are B. G., type **bglink**

3 Click the OK button.

Preview the lesson

The presentation for this lesson contains reference information about linking information with other applications. To preview the information in this lesson, click the Slide Show button on the Toolbar and view the on-screen presentation.

Slide Show

1 On the Toolbar, click the Slide Show button.

PowerPoint displays the first slide in the presentation.

2 Click to advance to the next slide.

3 Click once for each slide to advance through the rest of the presentation.

After the last slide in the presentation, PowerPoint returns to the current view.

Change to the next slide

▶ Click the down arrow on the Slide Changer to advance to slide 2.

Linking and Embedding in this Lesson

For some sections in this lesson, you'll need the Windows application Microsoft Excel version 4.0 or later. If you don't have this application, you can use the same techniques with other Windows applications that support linking and embedding, or read the sections to learn the concepts.

Linking to a Document

To ensure your presentation always shows the latest information, you can create a link between a source document, such as a Microsoft Excel chart document, and your PowerPoint presentation. To create a link, select the source document information you want to link, choose the Copy command, return to your PowerPoint presentation, and choose the Paste Special command.

Link a chart from Microsoft Excel to a slide

1 Press CTRL+ESC to display the Task List.

The Task List dialog appears.

2 Select the Program Manager and click the Switch To button.

For information on Microsoft Excel, see the Microsoft Excel documentation.

3 Locate and start Microsoft Excel.

4 Open the Microsoft Excel chart document LINKCHRT.XLC.

Make sure the PRACTICE directory is open. If it is not, select the drive where the Step by Step practice files are stored and open the appropriate directories. If you do not see LINKCHRT.XLC in the list of file names, check to be sure the correct drive and directory are selected. If you need help, see "Getting Ready."

5 Click the OK button.

A dialog box appears asking you to update references to unopened documents.

6 Click the No button.

7 From the Chart menu, choose Select Chart.

8 From the Edit menu, choose Copy (CTRL+C).

A selection box appears around the chart.

9 Switch to your PowerPoint presentation.

Tip   For a quick way to switch to PowerPoint or any other Windows application, hold down the ALT key and then press the TAB key. A billboard with an application icon and name appears. Continue to press the TAB key until the PowerPoint icon and name appear. Release the ALT and TAB keys to switch to PowerPoint.

---

10 From the Edit menu, choose Paste Special.

The Paste Special dialog box appears.

Be sure Microsoft Excel Chart Object is selected here . . .

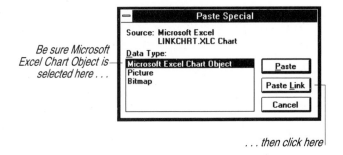

. . . then click here

The Paste Special dialog box displays a list of different data types to which the object on the Windows Clipboard can be pasted to a PowerPoint slide. The selected data type, Microsoft Excel Chart Object, is the data type currently placed on the Windows Clipboard.

11 Click the Paste Link button.

The Microsoft Excel chart appears on the PowerPoint slide.

Editing a Link to a Document

Once a link is created, you decide how information updates, either automatically or manually. All links are initially set as automatic links. You can change a link in a destination document from automatic to manual, so that you can control when the information updates. You may want to make a link manual if the link does not need to be updated very often or if you have several links in the document. Manual links are not updated from the source document until you request an update.

Update an automatically linked Microsoft Excel chart

1   Double-click the Microsoft Excel chart.

The Microsoft Excel chart appears.

2   Click the 3-D Pie Chart button at the bottom of the Microsoft Excel Window.

The Microsoft Excel chart changes to a 3-D pie chart.

3   Switch back to PowerPoint.

Use ALT+TAB to switch applications. The Microsoft Excel chart automatically updates to show a pie chart.

Change an automatic link to a manual link

1   From the Edit menu, choose Links.

The Links dialog box appears.

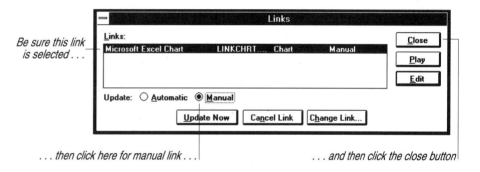

Be sure this link is selected . . .

. . . then click here for manual link . . .   *. . . and then click the close button*

The Links dialog box shows the current type of linked file, name of the file, and the type of link, automatic or manual.

2   Click the Manual option button.

The type of link changes from automatic to manual. The next time the Microsoft Excel chart changes, PowerPoint will not automatically update the chart to your presentation.

3   Click the Close button.

Update a manually linked Microsoft Excel chart

1   Double-click the Microsoft Excel chart.

The Microsoft Excel chart appears.

2 Click the 3-D Column Chart button at the bottom of the Microsoft Excel Window.

The Microsoft Excel chart changes to a column chart.

3 Switch back to PowerPoint.

Use ALT+TAB to switch applications. The Microsoft Excel chart doesn't update.

4 From the Edit menu, choose Links.

Tip   To update more than one link, hold down the CTRL key and click each link. To update a contiguous set of links, select the first link and then hold down the SHIFT key and select the last link.

---

5 Click the Update Now button.

An update link status message appears. The link to the chart updates.

6 Click the Close button.

The Microsoft Excel chart updates. Your presentation window should look similar to the following illustration:

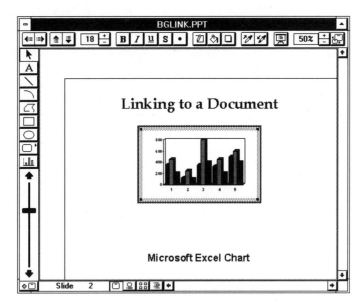

7 Switch to Microsoft Excel.

Use ALT+TAB to switch applications.

8 From the File menu, choose Exit.

Another update dialog box appears.

9   Click the No button to ignore changes to LINKCHRT.XLC.

A close dialog box appears. (Remote Links to a document exist.)

10   Click the OK button.

PowerPoint becomes active.

Change to the next slide

▶   Click the down arrow on the Slide Changer to advance to slide 3.

Linking a Picture

Pictures from other applications can be linked to a PowerPoint slide. Changes made to a linked picture are sent automatically to PowerPoint as soon as they are available. This ensures that your presentation always shows the latest information.

Link a picture to a slide

1   From the Edit menu, choose Insert, and then choose Picture.

The Insert Picture dialog box appears. (This dialog box functions just like the Open dialog box.)

2   In the Directories box, be sure the PRACTICE directory is open. If it is not, select the drive where the Step by Step practice files are stored and open the appropriate directories to find the PRACTICE directory.

3   In the list of file names, click LOGO1.TIF.

If you do not see LOGO1.TIF in the list of file names, check to be sure the correct drive and directory are selected. If you need help, see "Getting Ready."

4   Click the Link to File check box.

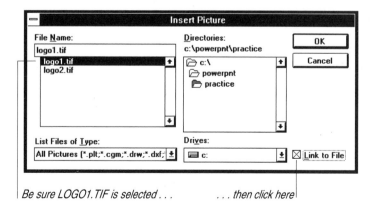

Be sure LOGO1.TIF is selected . . .   . . . then click here

An **X** in the Link to File check box creates a link to the picture, LOGO1.TIF.

5   Click the OK button.

Your presentation window should look similar to the following illustration:

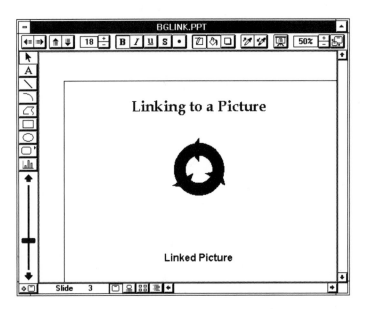

Change a link

When you paste and link data into a PowerPoint presentation, PowerPoint attaches the path and name of the source document to the linked information. The destination application uses this information to locate the source data that appears in your document. If you change the name of the source document or move the source document to a different directory or network drive, you must change the links to include the new name or path of the source document.

1   From the Edit menu, choose Links.

The Links dialog box appears.

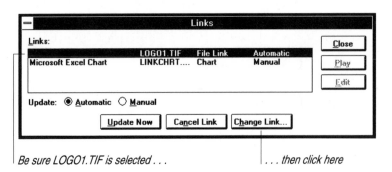

2   Click the Change Link button.

3   In the Directories box, be sure the PRACTICE directory is open. If it is not, select the drive where the Step by Step practice files are stored and open the appropriate directories to find the PRACTICE directory.

4   In the list of file names, select LOGO2.TIF.

5   Click the OK button.

6   Click the Update Now button.

An update link status message appears. The link to the picture changes from LOGO1.TIF to LOGO2.TIF

7   Click the Close button.

Your presentation window should look similar to the following illustration:

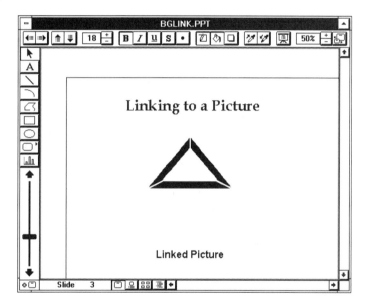

Cancel a link

You might want to cancel a link permanently so that the information in the destination document no longer updates from the source document.

1   From the Edit menu, choose Links.

The Links dialog box appears. The link to LOGO2.TIF is selected.

2   Click the Cancel Link button.

The link is removed from the list.

3   Click the Close button.

Change to the next slide

▶ Click the down arrow on the Slide Changer to advance to slide 4.

Embedding an Object

You can embed an object into a PowerPoint slide to create a direct link with an application that can be edited from your presentation. Simply double-click the embedded object on your PowerPoint slide to edit it, and choose Exit to return to PowerPoint. The changes you have made to the embedded object are made on your PowerPoint slide.

Embed a Microsoft Excel object on a slide

1 From the Edit menu, choose Insert, and then choose Object.

The Insert Object dialog box appears. The Insert Object dialog box shows the currently installed applications that can be embedded into your presentation.

2 Select Microsoft Excel Worksheet.

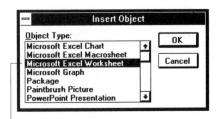

Be sure the Microsoft Excel Worksheet is selected

3 Click the OK button.

A Microsoft Excel worksheet appears entitled, Worksheet in BGLINK.PPT.

For information on creating a Microsoft Excel worksheet, see the Microsoft Excel documentation.

4 Type the following text in the Microsoft Excel worksheet as shown below.

	A	B	C	D	E
1		March	April	May	Total
2	Widgets	412	522	653	1587
3	Sprockets	400	390	460	1250
4	Cogs	240	350	330	920
5	Mallets	375	495	803	1673

Use the Arrow Keys to move among cells.

5 From the File menu, choose Exit.

An update dialog box appears.

6 Click the Yes button to update the worksheet in BGLINK.PPT.

The Worksheet appears on the PowerPoint slide. Since the slide view scale is set to 50%, the worksheet appears small. You'll use the scale command to enlarge the worksheet.

7 From the Object menu, choose Scale.

8 Type **200** in the Scale To box.

9 Click the OK button.

The worksheet scales 200 percent.

Update an embedded Microsoft Excel object

1 Double-click the embedded Microsoft Excel worksheet.

Microsoft Excel opens to the Worksheet in BGLINK.PPT.

2 Select cell B3.

3 Type **350**

4 From the File menu, choose Exit.

An update dialog box appears.

5 Click the Yes button.

The Excel Worksheet updates the PowerPoint slide with the change you just made.

Print the quick-reference notebook presentation

For information on printing a presentation, refer to Lesson 13.

1 From the File menu, choose Print (CTRL+P).

The Print dialog box appears.

2 Click the down arrow next to the Print box.

3 Click Handouts (2 slides per page) from the drop-down list.

4 Click the OK button.

A dialog box appears to give your printing status.

Save the Presentation

▶ From the File menu, choose Save (CTRL+S).

A dialog box doesn't appear, because the presentation already has a name. The current information in your presentation is saved with the same name.

One Step Further

You have learned how to create a link to a document and picture, update, change, and cancel a link, and embed an object to a PowerPoint slide. If you'd like to practice these and other basic skills in your practice presentation, try the following:

▶ Create a link to Microsoft Paintbrush. Open and close documents and presentations with links.

▶ Create, change and cancel links to pictures.

▶ Insert other Objects that exist on your system.

If you want to continue to the next lesson

1 From the File menu, choose Close (CTRL+F4).

2 If a dialog box appears asking if you want to save the changes to your presentation, choose the No button. You do not need to save the changes you made to the presentation after you printed it.

Choosing this command closes the active presentation; it does not exit PowerPoint. If no other presentations are open, the menu bar displays two available menus: File and Help.

If you want to quit PowerPoint for now

1 From the File menu, choose Exit.

2 If a dialog box appears asking if you want to save changes to the presentation, click the No button.

Lesson Summary

To	Do this
Link to a document	Switch to the document. Copy the information. Switch to PowerPoint. From the Edit menu, choose Paste Special. Click the Paste Link button.
Edit a link to a document	Double-click the document in PowerPoint. Make changes to the document. From the File menu, choose Exit.
Change a link to automatic or manual	From the Edit menu, choose Links. Select the link. Click the Automatic or Manual option button.

To	Do this
Link a picture	From the Edit menu, choose Insert, and then choose Picture. Select a picture. Click the Link to File check box.
Redirect a link	From the Edit menu, choose Links. Click the Change Link button. Select the new file to link. Click the Update Now button.
Cancel a link	From the Edit menu, choose Links. Select the link. Click the Cancel Link button.
Embed an object	From the Edit menu, choose Insert, and then choose Object. Select object to embed. Input information in the document. From the File menu, choose Exit.

For more information on	See the *Microsoft PowerPoint Handbook*
Inserting Information into PowerPoint	Chapter 12, "Using PowerPoint with Other Applications"

Preview of the Next Lesson

In the next lesson, you'll print presentation slides, speaker's notes pages, audience handouts, and an outline. By the end of the lesson, you'll have produced another presentation for your quick-reference notebook.

Part 6

Printing and Producing a Presentation

Setting Up Your Slides and Printing

PowerPoint printing allows you to print your presentation slides, speaker's notes, audience handouts, or outline. PowerPoint also includes a way to create an output file that can be sent to a service bureau for imaging to 35mm slides. Printing in PowerPoint offers a number of options: paper size, page orientation, range of pages, printers, and several output alternatives.

In this lesson, you'll learn how to choose a printer, change a slide format using the slide options, set up a presentation for printing, and print slides, speaker's notes, an outline and audience handouts. At the end of the lesson, your presentation will consist of the following slides:

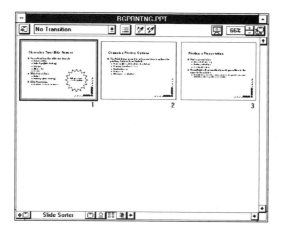

This lesson explains how to do the following:

- Choose a printer
- Change a presentation slide format
- Print presentation slides
- Print speaker's notes
- Print an outline of slide titles and bodies
- Print audience handouts

Estimated lesson time: 30 minutes

Open a presentation

If you haven't already started PowerPoint, do so now. For information about starting PowerPoint, see "Getting Ready," earlier in this book.

1   From the File menu, choose Open (CTRL+O).

2   In the Directories box, be sure the PRACTICE directory is open. If it is not, select the drive where the Step by Step practice files are stored and open the appropriate directories to find the PRACTICE directory.

For information about opening a sample presentation, refer to Lesson 2.

3   In the list of file names, click LESSON13.PPT.

If you do not see LESSON13.PPT in the list of file names, check to be sure the correct drive and directory are selected. If you need help, see "Getting Ready."

4   Click the OK button.

Your presentation opens to the following slide:

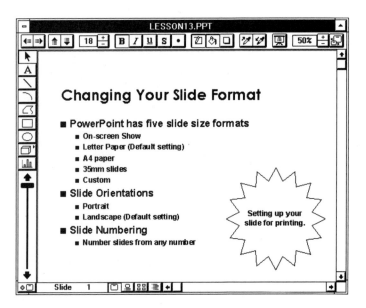

Save the presentation with a new name

Give the presentation a new name so the changes you make in this lesson will not overwrite the original presentation.

1   From the File menu, choose Save As.

2   In the File Name box, type *your initials***prntng**

For example, if your initials are B.G., type **bgprntng**

3   Click the OK button.

Preview the lesson

The presentation for this lesson contains reference information about setting up your slides and printing. To preview the information in this lesson, click the Slide Show button on the Toolbar and view the on-screen presentation.

Slide Show

1 On the Toolbar, click the Slide Show button.

PowerPoint displays the first slide in the presentation.

2 Click to advance to the next slide.

3 Click once for each slide to advance through the rest of the presentation.

After the last slide in the presentation, PowerPoint returns to the current view.

Choosing a Printer

Presentations print to the default printer unless you select a special printer. Your default printer is set up in the Windows Control Panel. You can choose a printer other than the default printer for slides and for notes, handouts, and outlines.

1 Make sure your printer is turned on and connected to your computer.

2 From the File menu, choose Print Setup.

The Print Setup dialog box appears.

If your printer does not show here . . .

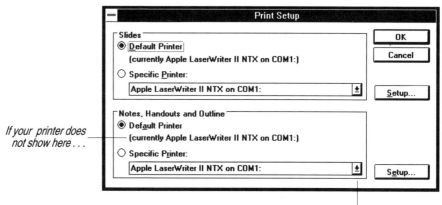

. . . then click here and select your printer from the drop-down list

Make sure your default printer is listed in the Slides box and Notes, Handouts and Outline box. If you don't want to use the current default printer, then click the drop-down arrow for the Specific Printer and select another printer.

TROUBLESHOOTING: **If your printer is not available in the drop-down list in the Specific Printer box**
See Appendix B, "Installing and Selecting a Printer," for information on how to install and select a printer.

3 Click the OK button.

Changing a Slide Format

The slide format determines the size and orientation of your printed slides. For a new presentation, PowerPoint opens with default slide format settings: Letter Paper (10 inches wide by 7.5 inches tall), landscape orientation, and slide numbers starting at one. If you need to change these slide format settings, it's a good idea to set the slide format before you design your presentation. Changing orientation or slide size for an existing presentation might change the scaling of objects on the slide.

Change the slide size and orientation

1 From the File menu, choose Slide Setup.

The Slide Setup dialog box appears.

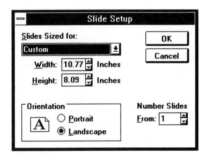

2 In the Slide Sized For box, click the drop-down arrow and select Letter Paper (8.5 x 11in).

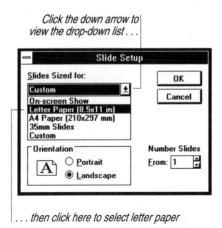

Click the down arrow to view the drop-down list . . .

. . . then click here to select letter paper

PowerPoint has four other slide size formats to choose from: On-screen Show, Letter Paper, A4 Paper, 35mm Slides and Custom.

- **On-screen Show**   Use this setting when designing an on-screen presentation or printing overhead transparencies on US letter paper.

- **Letter Paper**   Use this setting when designing a presentation for US letter paper (8.5 x 11 in).

- **A4 Paper**   Use this setting when printing to (international) A4 paper (210 x 297 mm) or (10.83 x 7.5 in).

- **35mm Slides**   Use this setting when designing a presentation for 35mm slides.

- **Custom**   Use this setting when designing a presentation with a special size. Select the height and width of the slide by clicking the arrow buttons up or down or positioning the cursor and typing a size. Anytime the height and width numbers do not match one of the three standard sizes, the format is a custom size format.

Note   The slide orientation should not be changed from landscape (7.5 x 10 in) to portrait (10 x 7.5 in) for existing presentations, because objects on the slides will shift or
scale to the new slide size. Slide orientation should be changed at the beginning of a new presentation.

---

3   Click the OK button.

A dialog box appears, indicating you might need to edit all your slides to the new size format.

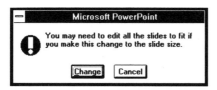

4   Click the Change button.

All the slides in your presentation now have the new slide size.

Your presentation window should look similar to the following illustration:

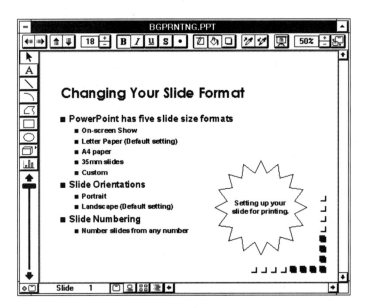

Change to the next slide

▶   Click the down arrow on the Slide Changer to advance to slide 2.

Printing in PowerPoint

PowerPoint allows you to print your presentation in four different ways: slides, speaker's notes, audience handouts, or an outline. A printing sample of your practice presentation looks similar to the following illustrations:

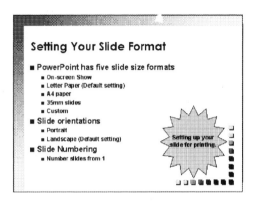

Slide (landscape)

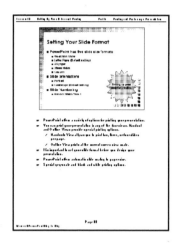

Notes Page

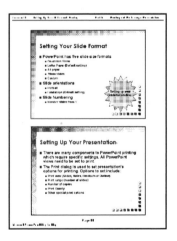

Handouts Page

Outline

Printing Slides, Notes, Handouts, and Outlines

You can print slides, audience handouts, speaker's notes, and your outline as it appears in Outline view using the Print command from the File menu. The Print dialog box allows you to specify print options such as what to print, print range, number of copies, print back and white, and scale to fit paper.

Printing Presentation Slides

In PowerPoint, your presentation slides automatically scale to the printer you have selected. Using scalable fonts such as TypeType allows you to print your presentation on different printers with the same great results.

Print slides

1 From the File menu, choose Print.

The Print dialog box appears.

2 Click the drop-down arrow next to the Print box.

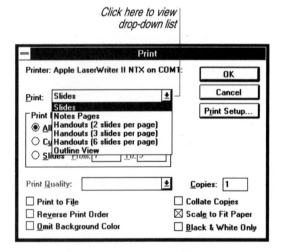

Click here to view drop-down list

Six print format options are available.

- **Slides**   Prints your slides as they appear on the screen, one per page.

- **Notes Pages**   Prints the speaker's notes pages that correspond with the slide numbers selected in the Print Range box.

- **Handouts (2 slides per page)**   Prints two slides per page.

- **Handouts (3 slides per page)**   Prints three slides per page.

- **Handouts (6 slides per page)**   Prints six slides per page.

- **Outline View**   Prints your outline according to your view scale setting. You can print titles and bodies, titles only, and draft mode.

For information about slide builds, refer to Lesson 15.

Note   If your presentation contains slides with build points, the Slides print option changes to Slides (with builds) and Slides (without builds). The Slides (with Builds) option prints each build point on a separate page. The Slides (without Builds) prints the complete slide on one page.

3   Select the Slides printing option to close the drop-down list.

4   Click the OK button.

A print dialog box appears to give your printing status.

Printing Speaker's Notes

You can print speaker's notes in the same way you print presentation slides. A reduced image of the presentation slide prints on each notes page.

Print speaker's notes with options

1   From the File menu, choose Print.

The Print dialog box appears.

2   Click the drop-down arrow next to the Print box and select Notes Pages.

3   In the Print Range box, click the Current Slide option button.

4   Click the Black & White check box.

Six print options are available at the bottom of the dialog box.

- **Print to File**   Use this option to print slides to a presentation file to create 35mm slides using a personal film recorder. This option could also be used to send a presentation to a Genigraphics service center. See Lesson 14, "Producing 35mm Slides" for more information on the Genigraphics.

- **Reverse Print Order**   Use this option to print from the last page to the first.

- **Omit Background Color**   Use this option to print without the background color on your slides, handouts, outlines, or notes. Shaded objects, however, retain their shading when printed. This option prints your presentation faster.

- **Collate Copies**   Use this option to print multiple copies of your presentation in reverse order so they are numerically organized out of the printer. This option is usually available on laser printers only.

Tip   When printing multiple copies of your presentation, turn the Collate Copies printing option off for faster results.

- **Scale to Fit Printer**   Use this option to scale slides automatically to fit the paper size in the printer. Use this only if the paper in the printer does not correspond to the slide size and orientation settings.

- **Black & White Only**   Turns all fills and colors white and all text and lines black. Use this option when printing draft copies of your presentation.

5   Click the OK button.

A print dialog box appears to give you printing status.

Printing an Outline

PowerPoint prints the outline of your presentation as it appears in Outline view. The text format and current view scale you see on-screen in Outline view is what you'll get when the outline prints. The current view of your presentation will not affect the print out.

Print an outline of your presentation

1   From the View menu, choose Outline.

View Scale

2   On the Toolbar, click the View Scale (+) button to increase the view to 50%.

3   From the File menu, choose Print.

The Print dialog box appears.

4   Click the drop-down arrow next to the Print box.

5   Select Outline View from the drop-down list.

6   In the Print Range box, click the All option button.

7   Click the Black & White check box to turn off the option.

8   Click the OK button.

A print dialog box appears to give your printing status.

9   Click the Slide View button.

Print Handout Pages

You can print Handouts in three different formats: 2 slides per page, 3 slides per page, and 6 slides per page. Add the handouts you'll print to your quick-reference notebook.

Print the quick-reference notebook presentation

1   From the File menu, choose Print (CTRL+P).

The Print dialog box appears.

2   Click the down arrow next to the Print box.

3   Click Handouts (2 slides per page) from the drop-down list.

4   Click the OK button.

A dialog box appears to give your printing status.

Save the presentation

▶ From the File menu, choose Save.

A dialog box doesn't appear because the presentation already has a name. The current information in your presentation is saved with the same name.

One Step Further

You have learned in this lesson to set your slide format and set up your presentation for printing. If you'd like to practice these and other basic skills in your practice presentation, try the following:

▶ From the Slides Sized for box, select A4 Paper, change the orientation or the width and height settings, and look at your slide to see what changed.

▶ Print your practice presentation using the different print options from the Print dialog box found in the File menu.

▶ Print your presentation in the different views: Notes, Handouts, Outline, and Slides with and without Builds.

If you want to continue to the next lesson

1 From the File menu, choose Close (CTRL+F4).

2 If a dialog box appears asking if you want to save the changes to your presentation, click the No button. You do not need to save the changes you made to the presentation after you printed it.

Choosing this command closes the active presentation; it does not exit PowerPoint. If no other presentations are open, the menu bar displays two available menus: File and Help.

If you want to quit PowerPoint for now

1 From the File menu, choose Exit.

2 If a dialog box appears asking if you want to save changes to the presentation, choose the No button.

Lesson Summary

To	Do this
Choose a printer	From the File menu, choose Print. Click the Print Setup button. Select a printer.
Change the slide format	From the File menu, choose Slide Setup and then select a slide format.
Print slides	From the File menu, choose Print. Click the Print drop-down arrow and select Slides.
Print notes pages	From the File menu, choose Print. Click the Print drop-down arrow and select Notes Pages.
Print audience handouts	From the File menu, choose Print. Click the Print drop-down arrow and select handouts (2, 3, or 6 slides per page).
Print an outline	From the File menu, choose Print. Click the Print drop-down arrow and select Outline view.
Print a black and white presentation	From the File menu, choose Print. Click the Black & White check box.
Print the current slide	From the File menu, choose Print. Click the Current Slide option button.

For more information on	See the *Microsoft PowerPoint Handbook*
Setting up slides for printing	Chapter 13, "Printing"

Preview of the Next Lesson

In the next lesson, you'll learn how to produce 35mm slides, how you save your presentation with the Genigraphics Driver, and how to send a presentation to Genigraphics using the GraphicsLink application. By the end of the lesson, you'll have produced another presentation for your quick-reference notebook.

Producing 35mm Slides

PowerPoint has made the process of producing 35mm slides from your presentation easier than ever. Your PowerPoint application connects to Genigraphics, a computer graphics company, that can produce professional 35mm slides from your presentation. You can send your presentation by way of modem or disk to a Genigraphics Service Center that will image your PowerPoint slides directly to 35mm color slides.

In this lesson, you'll learn how to select the Genigraphics driver, set slide and Genigraphics print options, and complete job instructions and billing information. You'll also start GraphicsLink and send a presentation file. At the end of the lesson, your presentation will consist of the following slides:

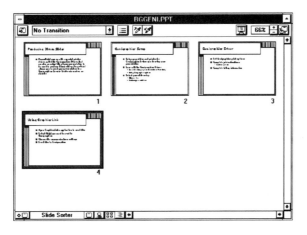

This lesson explains how to do the following:

- Select the Genigraphics Driver
- Set slide and Genigraphics print options
- Complete job instructions and billing information
- Open and send files with GraphicsLink

Estimated lesson time: 25 minutes

Open a presentation

If you haven't already started PowerPoint, do so now. For instructions about starting PowerPoint, see "Getting Ready," earlier in this book.

1 From the File menu, choose Open (CTRL+O).

2 In the Directories box, be sure the PRACTICE directory is open. If it is not, select the drive where the Step by Step practice files are stored and open the appropriate directories to find the PRACTICE directory.

For information about opening a sample presentation, refer to Lesson 2.

3 In the list of file names, select LESSON14.PPT.

If you do not see LESSON14.PPT in the list of file names, check to be sure the correct drive and directory are selected. If you need help, see "Getting Ready."

4 Click the OK button.

Your presentation opens to the following slide:

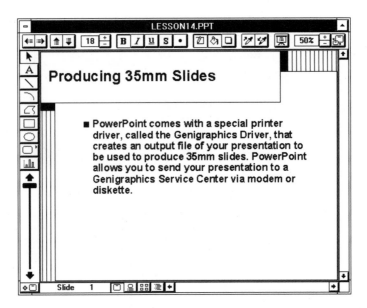

Save the presentation with a new name

Give the presentation a new name so the changes you make in this lesson will not overwrite the original presentation.

1 From the File menu, choose Save As.

2 In File Name box, type *your initials***geni**

For example, if your initials are B. G., type **bggeni**

3 Click the OK button.

Preview the lesson

The presentation for this lesson contains reference information about Genigraphics. To preview the information in this lesson, click the Slide Show button on the Toolbar and view the presentation.

Slide Show

1   On the Toolbar, click the Slide Show button.

PowerPoint displays the first slide in the presentation.

2   Click to advance to the next slide.

3   Click once for each slide to advance through the rest of the presentation.

After the last slide in the presentation, PowerPoint returns to the current view.

Change to the next slide

▶   Click the down arrow on the Slide Changer to advance to slide 2.

Setting Up the Genigraphics Driver

Before you send your presentation to a Genigraphics Service Center, you must set the appropriate PowerPoint settings. PowerPoint comes with a special printer driver, called the Genigraphics Driver, which you must select before you can send your presentation. Selecting the Genigraphics Driver includes choosing specific options, which are designed to make the process easier.

The Genigraphics Driver and setup options

1   From the File menu, choose Print Setup.

The Print Setup dialog box appears.

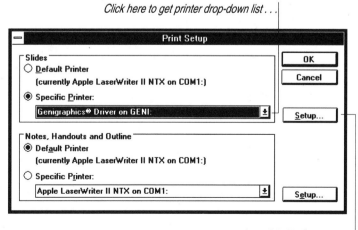

Click here to get printer drop-down list . . .

. . . then click this Setup button

2 In the Slides box, click the down arrow next to the Specific Printer box and select the Genigraphics® Driver on GENI.

The Genigraphics Driver sets the aspect ratio and image size of the slides.

3 Click the Setup button to the right of the Specific Printer drop-down list in the Slides box.

The Genigraphics Setup dialog box appears.

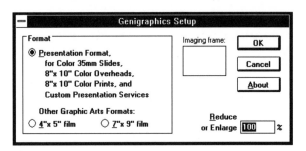

TROUBLESHOOTING: **If you click the wrong Setup button** A setup dialog box appears for printing to a regular printer. Click the Cancel button to return to the Print Setup dialog box and repeat step 3.

The Genigraphics Setup dialog box allows you to choose from three Genigraphics formats. **Do not** change the default format setting.

- **Presentation format** Use this format for 35mm slides, 8" x 10" overheads and prints, and custom presentations.

- **4" x 5" film** Use this setting when you want to work with color on printing materials, such as brochures.

- **7" x 9" film** Used this format when you want enlarge your presentation for display.

Tip To prepare an existing presentation for Genigraphics, select Presentation Format in the Genigraphics Setup dialog box.

---

4 Click the OK button.

The Print Setup dialog box reappears.

5 Click the OK button.

Slide setup

1 From the File menu, choose Slide Setup.

The Slide Setup dialog box appears.

2 In the Slides Sized for box, click the down arrow and select 35mm Slides.

Click here to get drop-down list

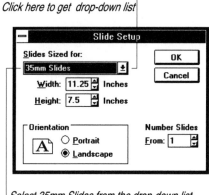

Select 35mm Slides from the drop-down list

3 Click the OK button.

An edit dialog box appears telling you your slides might need to be edited.

4 Click the Change button.

Your presentation is now ready to be saved with the Genigraphics Driver.

Fit the slide to the window

▶ From the Window menu, choose Fit to Page Size.

Your presentation window expands to encompass the larger slide format.

Change to the next slide

▶ Click the down arrow on the Slide Changer to advance to slide 3.

Creating a Genigraphics Presentation

Your presentation has been created and is ready to save to the Genigraphics Driver. To save your presentation, you need to select print options as you would for any other printing driver. However, saving with the Genigraphics Driver requires you to fill out job instructions and billing information.

Save your presentation to create 35mm slides

1   From the File menu, choose Print (CTRL+P).

The Print dialog box appears, displaying Slides in the Print box and the Genigraphics Driver on GENI as the currently selected printer.

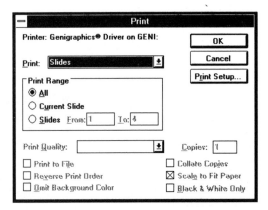

TROUBLESHOOTING: **If your Print dialog does not look like the dialog box show above**   Click the Print Setup button and follow the steps under the "Genigraphics Setup" section, earlier in this lesson.

2   In the Print Range box, click the All option button, if not already selected.

All the other settings in the Print dialog box are set correctly.

3   Click the OK button.

The Genigraphics Job Instructions dialog box appears. This dialog provides Genigraphics with instructions on how to process your order.

4   In the Copies box next to 8"x 10" Overheads, double-click the 0.

5   Type **2**

The information in the Copies box tells Genigraphics to send you one set of 35mm slides on plastic mounts and two sets of 8" x 10" overheads.

6   Insert a blank, formatted disk into drive A or (B).

7   In the Send Via box, click the Diskette option button.

This option saves your presentation as a Genigraphics file to a diskette.

8   In the Return Via box, click the Mail option button.

Your order will be returned to you through the mail when Genigraphics has completed the necessary work.

9   In the Save As box, double-click BGGENI and type **Project1**

The Genigraphics Job Instructions dialog box should look similar to the following illustration:

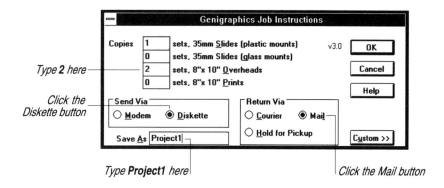

Note   You can customize your Genigraphics order by clicking the Custom button in the Genigraphics Job Instructions dialog box.

10   Click the OK button.

The standard Save As dialog box appears because you selected a diskette. Selecting the modem option in the Genigraphics Job Instructions dialog box would save your file to the Genigraphics directory in your Windows 3.1 system folder.

11   In the Drives box, click the down arrow and select A (or B, depending on where your diskette is located).

12   Click the OK button.

A print status dialog appears, and then the Genigraphics Billing Information dialog box appears.

Billing information

The Genigraphics Billing Information dialog box requires you to fill in information for your Genigraphics Service Center.

To successfully complete saving your presentation, enter the required basic information. The small "x" located to the left of some boxes identifies information that is always required by the Genigraphics Service Center.

1   Type **Widgets Int.** in the Company box and press TAB.

2   Type **KLB** in the Contact box and press TAB twice.

3   Type **123 Main St.** in the Street Address box and press TAB twice.

4   Type **Anywhere** in the City box and press TAB.

5   Type **CA** in the State box and press TAB.

6   Type **91234** in the Zip box and press TAB.

7   Type **(510) 555-1234**

8   In the Billing box, click the COD option button.

The Genigraphics Billing Information dialog box should look similar to the following illustration:

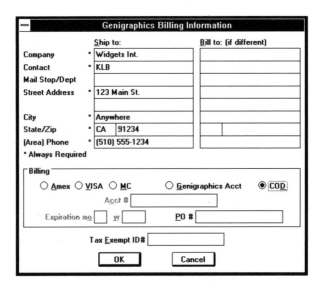

9   Click the OK button.

A Genigraphics Driver dialog box appears, telling you your presentation has been saved with the file name PROJECT1.GNA.

10 Click the OK button.

Your presentation saves on the disk and can now be sent to the Genigraphics Service Center of your choosing.

Change to the next slide

▶ Click the down arrow on the Slide Changer to advance to slide 4.

Using GraphicsLink

GraphicsLink is a telecommunications program which comes with PowerPoint that enables you to send your presentation file by modem to a Genigraphics Service Center. GraphicsLink allows you to keep track of all presentation files, their job descriptions, and billing information.

Switch to the Program Manager

1   Press CTRL+ESC to display the Task List.

The Task List dialog box appears. PowerPoint is still open. More than one application can be open at the same time.

2   Select the Program Manager and click the Switch To button.

Start GraphicsLink and select your file

1   Double-click the GraphicsLink icon from the Microsoft PowerPoint program group window.

The GraphicsLink window appears.

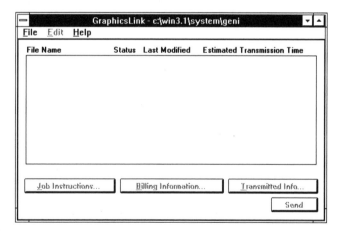

2 From the GraphicsLink File menu, choose Switch Directory (CTRL+D).

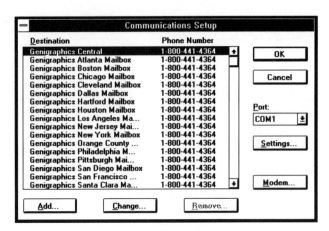

Click the drive where your diskette is located . . .

. . . then click here . . .

. . . and then click your file name here

3 In the Directories box, select [-a-] or [-b-], depending on where your disk is located.

4 Click the Open button.

5 In the Files box, select PROJECT1.GNA.

6 Click the OK button.

The GraphicsLink window displays your presentation.

Transmit your presentation

1 From the GraphicsLink File menu, choose Communications Setup.

The Communications Setup dialog box appears.

Note   To actually send your file to Genigraphics Service Center, use the Communications setup dialog box to select the phone line to transmit your file.

---

2   Click the Cancel button.

To actually send your presentation with the GraphicsLink application, click the Send button. A Send Status dialog box appears, showing you the progress of your transmission. After your transmission is final, a transmission summary appears on your screen, telling you the results of your transmission.

Note   When a file has been successfully transmitted to a Genigraphics Service Center, the GNA file is deleted and replaced with a .GNX file. This new file contains a job report and transmission summary report which gives you an accurate record of all your Genigraphics orders.

---

3   From the File menu choose Exit.

The GraphicsLink application closes.

4   Press CTRL+ESC to display the Task List.

The Task List dialog box appears.

5   Select Microsoft PowerPoint and click the Switch To button.

Print the quick-reference notebook presentation

1   From the File menu, choose Print.

The Print dialog box appears.

2   Click the down arrow next to the Print box.

3   Click Handouts (2 slides per page) in the drop-down list.

4   Click the OK button.

A print dialog box appears to give you printing status.

Save the Presentation

▶   From the File menu, choose Save (CTRL+S).

A dialog box doesn't appear, because the presentation already has a name. The current information in your presentation is saved with the same name.

One Step Further

You have learned to setup your slides and printer for Genigraphics, save a presentation file with Genigraphics format, set Genigraphics options, and use GraphicsLink to send your file. If you'd like to practice these and other basic skills in your practice presentation, try the following:

▶ Select the Modem option from the Send Via box in the Genigraphics Job Instructions dialog box. Find the file in the Windows directory.

▶ Prepare and send a presentation to a Genigraphics Service Center.

If you want to continue to the next lesson

1 From the File menu, choose Close (CTRL+F4).

2 If a dialog box appears asking if you want to save the changes to the presentation, click the No button.

If you want to quit PowerPoint for now

1 From the File menu, choose Exit.

2 If a dialog box appears asking if you want to save changes to the presentation, click the No button.

Lesson Summary

To	Do this
Select the Genigraphics Driver	From the File menu, choose Print Setup. Click the Specific Printer drop-down arrow and select Genigraphics Driver.
Select Genigraphics setup options	From the Print Setup dialog box, click the Setup button.
Setup Genigraphics slide options	From the File menu, choose Slide Setup. Select 35mm Slides.
Save your presentation with Genigraphics format	From the File menu, choose Print.
Fill out the Genigraphics Job Instructions dialog box	From the Print dialog box, click the OK button.
Fill out the Genigraphics Billing Information dialog box	From the Genigraphics Job Instructions dialog, click the OK button.
Use the GraphicsLink application	From the Program Manager, double-click the GraphicsLink icon.
Select your phone number and modem	From the GraphicsLink File menu, choose Communication Setup.

For more information on	See the **Using Microsoft PowerPoint and Genigraphics Presentation Services booklet**
Creating a 35mm presentation	"Using the Genigraphics® Driver"
Sending slides to Genigraphics	"Using GraphicsLink"

Preview of the Next Lesson

In the next lesson, you'll learn how to produce an electronic presentation by adding slide transitions and timings, build slides, rehearse timings, and use the PowerPoint Viewer. By the end of the lesson, you'll have produced another presentation for your quick-reference notebook.

Producing an Electronic Presentation

In PowerPoint you can display your presentation on your computer using Slide Show. The Slide Show feature turns your computer into a projector that displays your presentation slide by slide. A Slide Show can also operate continuously unattended to show a presentation.

In this lesson, you'll learn how to draw on a slide during a slide show, add slide transitions, and bullet point transitions called a *Build Slide*. You'll also set slide timings for slides, rehearse your slide show, and show presentations with the PowerPoint Viewer. At the end of the lesson, your presentation will consist of the following slides:

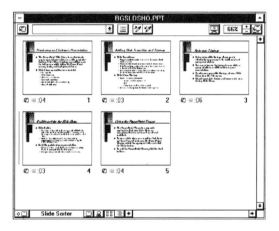

This lesson explains how to do the following:

- Freehand draw in slide show
- Set slide transitions and timings
- Rehearse a slide show
- Create a build slide
- Show presentations with the PowerPoint Viewer

Estimated lesson time: 20 minutes

Open a presentation

If you haven't already started PowerPoint, do so now. For instructions about starting PowerPoint, see "Getting Ready," earlier in this book.

1   From the File menu, choose Open (CTRL+O).

2   In the Directories box, be sure the PRACTICE directory is open. If it is not, select the drive where the Step by Step practice files are stored and open the appropriate directories to find the PRACTICE directory.

For information about opening a sample presentation, refer to Lesson 2.

3   In the list of file names, click LESSON15.PPT.

If you do not see LESSON15.PPT in the list of files names, check to be sure the correct drive and directory are selected. If you need help, see "Getting Ready."

4   Click the OK button.

Your presentation opens to the following slide:

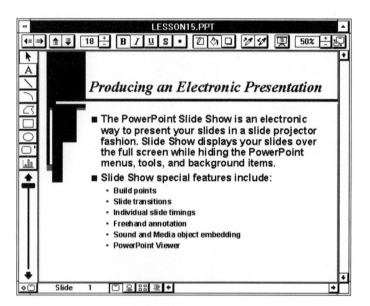

Save the presentation with a new name

Give the presentation a new name so the changes you make in this lesson will not overwrite the original document.

1   From the File menu, choose Save As.

2   In the File Name box, type *your initials***sldsho**

For example, if your initials are B. G., type **bgsldsho**

3   Click the OK button.

Freehand Drawing in Slide Show

During a slide show presentation, you can draw lines, circles and arrows to emphasize your message. Click and hold the mouse down, and then draw. When you finish drawing, release the mouse.

Draw a freehand line

Slide Show

1   On the Toolbar, click the Slide Show button.

PowerPoint displays the first slide in the presentation.

2   Position the pointer under the bullet in "PowerPoint Viewer."

"PowerPoint Viewer" is the last line on the slide.

3   Click and hold the mouse until you get a drawing point.

4   Draw a line under "PowerPoint Viewer."

TROUBLESHOOTING: **If you click and release the mouse button**   The slide show will proceed to the second slide. To use the freehand drawing, you must click *and hold* the mouse button. To get back to the first slide, press the LEFT ARROW key.

Slide show controls

1   Press the E key to erase the line you drew.

2   Press the A key to hide the arrow pointer.

You can press the A key again to show the arrow pointer.

3   Press the B key to black the screen.

4   Press the RIGHT ARROW key to advance to the next slide.

You can press the LEFT ARROW key to return to the previous slide.

Note   You can use the arrow keys on the ten-key pad if the NUM-LOCK key is not pressed. If it is pressed, the arrows on the ten-key pad have no effect.

---

5   Click once for each slide to advance through the rest of the presentation.

After the last slide in the presentation, PowerPoint returns to the current view.

Change to the next slide

▶   Click the down arrow on the Slide Changer to advance to slide 2.

Setting Slide Transitions and Timings

A slide transition is the visual effect given to a slide as it moves on and off the screen during a slide show. Slide transitions include such effects as Checkerboard Across, Cover Down, Cut, and Split Vertical Out; there are a total of 46 slide transition effects. You can set a transition for one slide or a group of slides by selecting the slide(s) and applying the transition.

Slide Timings refer to the time a slide appears on the screen. As with transitions, you can set slide timings for one slide or a group of slides depending on how many slides you have selected when you apply the slide timing.

Apply a slide transition

Slide Sorter

1   Click the Slide Sorter button.

2   On the Toolbar, click the down arrow next to the transition effect box.

3   Select Checkerboard Across.

Click here to view drop-down list . . .

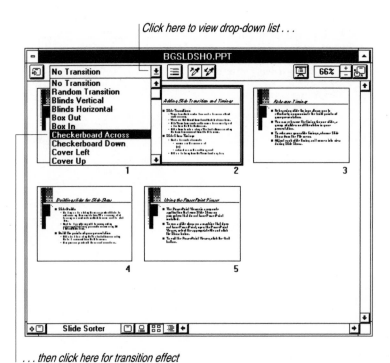

. . . then click here for transition effect

PowerPoint places a transition icon below the lower left corner of slide 2. This tells you a slide transition has been applied to this slide.

Slide Show

4   On the Toolbar, click the Slide Show button.

Slide Show displays slide 2 with the Checkerboard Across effect.

5   Press the ESC key.

PowerPoint returns you to slide 2.

Apply multiple transitions and timings

1   From the Edit menu, choose Select All (CTRL+A).

Transition Button

2   On the Toolbar, click the Transition button or from the Slide menu, choose Transition.

The Transition dialog box appears.

3   Click the down arrow under Effect, and select Random Transition.

The view box demonstrates the transition effect.

4   Click the Slow option button to set the transition speed.

5   In the Advance box, click the Automatically After—Seconds option button.

6   Type **4**

There are two ways to advance your slide show, by mouse click or automatically.

- The automatic advance timing feature moves your slide(s) through the Slide Show automatically, keeping the slide on the screen the length of time designated in the Advance box.

- The mouse click manually moves your slide(s) through the entire Slide Show.

The Transition dialog box should look similar to the following illustration:

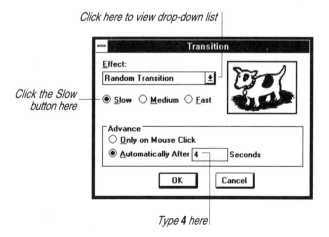

Click here to view drop-down list

Click the Slow button here

Type 4 here

Tip   A click will always advance a slide, even if the timing set in the transition box has not elapsed. Conversely, holding down the mouse button will prevent a timed transition from showing until you release the mouse, even if the set timing has elapsed.

7   Click the OK button.

All the slides of your presentation now have a transition icon and a slide time (:04) positioned below the left corner of the slides.

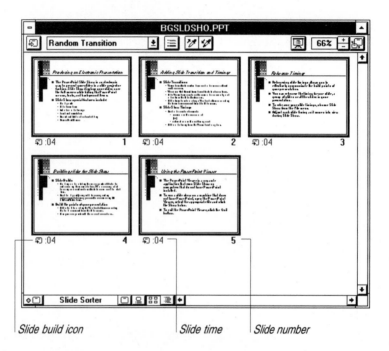

Slide build icon   *Slide time*   *Slide number*

Slide Show

8   On the Toolbar, click the Slide Show button.

Slide Show runs through your presentation, using the slide time and transition you set in the Transition dialog box.

Setting Rehearse Slide Timings

You can also set slide timings using the Rehearse Slide Timing command. If you are unsure of how fast to set the slide timings of your presentation, you can rehearse your slide show and adjust your timings appropriately for each slide.

1   From the File menu, choose Slide Show.

The Slide Show dialog box appears.

2   In the Advance box, click the Rehearse New Timings option button.

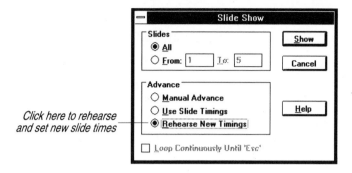

*Click here to rehearse
and set new slide times*

Note   Before you click the Show button in step three, read steps 3 and 4 completely to understand what you need to do when Slide Show begins.

---

3   Click the Show button.

Slide Show begins, displaying three time buttons in the lower left of the screen that look like the following illustration:

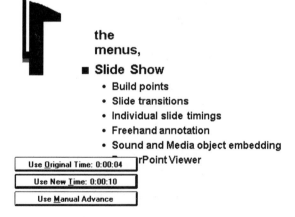

The Use New Time button begins running, as soon as the first slide appears.

- Click the Use Original Time button if the timing for that slide is adequate to read and view the information.

- Click the Use New Time button to apply a new time to a slide when the original time is insufficient to read the information on the slide.

- Click the Use Manual Advance button if you do not want an automatic timing for a particular slide.

4   Click the Use New Time button to select a new slide timings for each slide in the presentation.

At the end of the slide rehearsal, a Confirm dialog box appears.

5   Click the Yes button to save the new slide timings.

Your slides now display different slide time settings.

6   Click in a blank area to deselect the slides.

Setting Build Slides for a Slide Show

All bullet point subparagraphs move with the major bullet points.

In a Slide Show, you can have slide bullet points transition one at a time on the screen. The transition of each bullet point onto the slide is called a *Build Slide*. You can build bullet points for a slide show using 30 different transition effects to effectively communicate your presentation. The Build feature can be applied only in the Slide Sorter and Slide Views.

Create a build slide

1   Select slide 4.

Slide View

2   Click the Slide View button.

3   From the Slide menu, choose Build.

The Build dialog box appears.

4   Click the down arrow next to the color box on the Dim Previous Points box line, and select gray (GY6).

The bullet points will change to gray as they dim from view during your slide show as each new build point appears.

5   Click the down arrow next to the Effect check box.

6   Click the down scroll arrow and select the transition Dissolve.

Click here to view drop-down list for dim colors

Build
☒ **B**uild Body Text
☒ **D**im Previous Points: `GY6` ±
☒ **E**ffect: `Dissolve` ±
OK   Cancel

*Click here to view drop-down list
for build point transition effects*

7 Click the OK button.

8 From the File menu, choose Slide Show.

The Slide Show dialog box appears.

9 In the Slides box, click the From option button.

10 Press the TAB key to switch to the To text box and type **4**

The Slide Show dialog box should look similar to the following illustration:

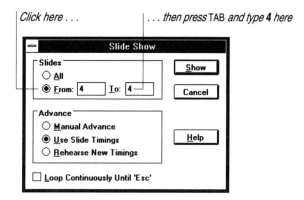

11 Click the Show button

Slide Show runs slide 4 with the new build effects, using the slide timing set in the slide show rehearsal.

Create multiple build slides

1 From the View menu, choose Slide Sorter.

2 From the Edit menu, choose Select All.

Build

3 On the Toolbar, click the Build Dialog button.

The Build dialog box appears. When multiple slides are selected with different settings, the Build dialog box indicates different settings by filling the option boxes with gray instead of an X. Selecting an option then sets all selected slides.

4 Click the down arrow next to the Dim Previous Points box, and select gray (GY6).

5 Click the down arrow next to the Effect check box, and select Random Transition.

6 Click the OK button.

All of the slides now have build icons below their lower left corners next to the transition icons, signifying they all have builds.

Note Applying builds to multiple slides might affect how long you want the slide to stay on the screen during a slide show. Slide timings are divided equally among the builds for each slide, and you might need to adjust the slide timing to adequately show your build points. For example, if you have a slide with four build points and a slide timing of 8 seconds, each build point will have 2 seconds on the screen.

Slide Show

7 On the Toolbar, click the Slide Show button.

The build slides appear during the on-screen presentation.

Using the PowerPoint Viewer

PowerPoint comes with a special application, called the PowerPoint Viewer, that allows you to show a slide show on a computer that does not have PowerPoint installed. You can freely copy the PowerPoint Viewer program onto any compatible system to allow you to run PowerPoint slide shows. To copy the program, use the File Manager application and copy PowerPoint Viewer onto a diskette.

Switch to the Program Manager

1 Press CTRL+ESC to display the Task List.

The Task List dialog box appears. PowerPoint is still open. More than one application can be open at the same time.

2 Select the Program Manager and click the Switch To button.

Showing Presentations with the PowerPoint Viewer

1 Double-click the PowerPoint Viewer icon from the Microsoft PowerPoint program group window.

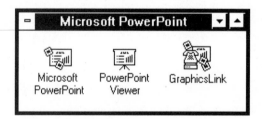

The Microsoft PowerPoint Viewer dialog box appears.

2 In the Directories box, be sure the PRACTICE directory is open. If it is not, select the drive where the Step by Step practice files are stored and open the appropriate directories to find the PRACTICE directory.

3 In the File Name box, select SLDSHOW1.PPT.

Use the up or down arrows in the scroll bar to find your practice presentation if you do not see it in the list.

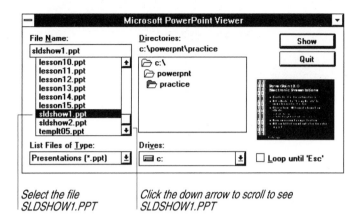

Select the file SLDSHOW1.PPT

Click the down arrow to scroll to see SLDSHOW1.PPT

4 Click the Show button.

PowerPoint shows SLDSHOW1.PPT—a presentation with PowerPoint samples—with the appropriate transitions, builds, and slide timings.

The PowerPoint Viewer responds to the same PowerPoint key and mouse commands. You have the same control over the Viewer as you have within PowerPoint.

When the slide show completes, the Microsoft PowerPoint Viewer dialog box reappears on your screen.

Show a list of presentations

With the PowerPoint Viewer, you can show multiple presentations, one after another with a playlist file. The playlist can contain Windows PowerPoint files, Macintosh PowerPoint files, and even other playlists (filename.lst). You can create a playlist file with the Windows Notepad application. Simply save the file with a (LST) extension.

1 Under List Files of Type, click the drop-down arrow.

2 Select File Lists (*.lst).

3 In the File Name box, select SHOWLIST.LST.

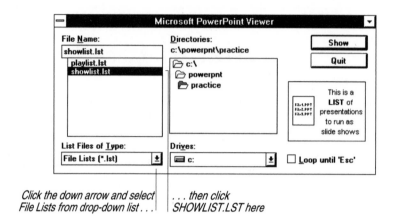

Click the down arrow and select | . . . then click
File Lists from drop-down list . . . | SHOWLIST.LST here

4 Click the Show button.

The PowerPoint Viewer shows SLDSHOW1.PPT and SLDSHOW2.PPT in order. To find out more about playlists, open the SHOWLIST.LST file with the Windows Notepad application.

5 Click the Quit button to exit the PowerPoint Viewer.

Switch back to PowerPoint

▶ Switch back to your PowerPoint presentation.

To switch to PowerPoint or any other Windows application, hold down the ALT key and press the TAB key. A billboard with an application icon and name appears. Continue to press the TAB key until the PowerPoint icon and name appear. Release the ALT key to switch to PowerPoint.

Print the quick-reference notebook presentation

For information on printing a presentation, refer to Lesson 13.

1 From the File menu, choose Print (CTRL+P).

The Print dialog box appears.

2 Click the down arrow next to the Print box.

3 Click Handouts (2 slides per page) from the drop-down list.

4 Click the OK button.

A dialog box appears to give your printing status.

Save the presentation

▶ From the File menu, choose Save (CTRL+S).

A dialog box doesn't appear, because the presentation already has a name. The current information in your presentation is saved with the same name.

One Step Further

You have learned to produce and present a slide show in PowerPoint using build points, transitions, and timings. If you'd like to practice these and other basic skills in your practice presentation, try the following:

▶ Practice freehand drawing and slide show commands during a slide show.

▶ Apply different transition and build effects to individual slides.

▶ Rehearse your presentation's slide timings with build slides.

▶ Use the PowerPoint Viewer to show your presentation on a compatible computer that does not have PowerPoint.

▶ Apply Transitions and Builds to other PowerPoint presentations.

If you want to quit PowerPoint for now

1 From the File menu, choose Exit.

2 If a dialog box appears asking if you want to save changes to the presentation, click the No button.

Lesson Summary

To	Do this
Freehand drawing in a slide show	Click the Slide Show button. Click and hold the mouse, and then draw.
Apply a slide transition	Select a slide(s). Click the Transition Dialog button on the Toolbar, or choose Transitions from the Slide menu.
Apply slide timings	From the Transition dialog box, choose either the manual or automatic setting.
Rehearse slide timings	From the File menu, choose Slide Show.
Apply a slide build	On the Toolbar, click the Build Dialog button.
Apply builds to multiple slides	Select more than one slide. On the Toolbar, click the Build Dialog button.
Run Slide Show	On the Toolbar, click the Slide Show button.
Stop a slide show	Press the ESC key.
Run the PowerPoint Viewer	Double-click the PowerPoint Viewer icon in the Program Manager.
Show more than one presentation in succession.	Create a playlist (*.lst) file with the Windows Notepad that includes a list of the presentation file names.

For more information on	See the *Microsoft PowerPoint Handbook*
Producing an Electronic Presentation	Chapter 14, "Giving a Slide Show on Your Computer"

Preview of the Next Section

Congratulations! You have completed all of the lessons in this book. You now have the skills you need to use Microsoft PowerPoint to create effective business presentations. If you need to brush up on specific tasks, you can repeat any of the lessons at any time.

In the appendixes that follow, you can learn how to install PowerPoint, and install and select a printer. You'll also find a list of the new features in Microsoft PowerPoint that are covered in this book, including the lessons in which they are used. For presenters on the go, who move presentations from computer to computer, Appendix D, "Presentations on the Go," gives you information to maximize your results. Appendix E contains a list of all the lessons and the associated PowerPoint presentation files.

Appendixes

Installing Microsoft PowerPoint

The Microsoft PowerPoint Setup program copies the PowerPoint program, the PowerPoint Viewer, the GraphicsLink program, and other files to your hard disk. Before you can start using PowerPoint, you must use the PowerPoint Setup program.

Hardware and Software Requirements

To use PowerPoint, your computer must meet the following minimum requirements:

- IBM PC or compatible with a 286, 386 or 486 processor. A 386 processor or higher
  is recommended.
- DOS 3.1 or later.
- Microsoft Windows graphical environment version 3.1 or later.
- 2 MB RAM (4 MB or more is recommended).
- IBM VGA, EGA, 8514, or any video adapter supported by Windows 3.1 (except CGA). A color monitor is recommended to take full advantage of the color features of PowerPoint.
- Optional: 256-color video adapter and compatible Microsoft Windows 3.1.
- Microsoft Mouse or other mouse compatible with Microsoft Windows 3.1.
- Hard disk plus one 5.25" 1.2 MB, or 3.5" 1.44 MB or 720 KB floppy drive.
- Optional: printer and/or film recorder compatible with Microsoft Windows 3.1.

Before You Install PowerPoint

Use the Windows 3.1 Setup program to install Windows on your computer before you install PowerPoint. With Windows Setup, you install screen fonts to display text on the screen and you install the printer driver for your printer. The printer driver provides your Windows-based programs with access to printer fonts and important instructions for your printer. When you set up Windows, you choose a printer port to establish a software connection between your computer and the printer. Finally, you choose the printer and the printer settings that you will use with the installed printer driver.

If you installed Windows without installing a printer, you must do so before you can print with PowerPoint. For information on installing a printer, check Appendix B, "Installing and Selecting a Printer" or refer to your Windows Setup documentation.

Using the PowerPoint Setup Program

The following Setup procedure covers the basics for setting up PowerPoint for the first time. For a detailed explanation of PowerPoint Setup, refer to your PowerPoint Setup documentation.

The following Setup procedure covers the basics for setting up PowerPoint. The options you choose during Setup determine the amount of disk space needed to install PowerPoint onto your hard disk.

Complete Installation   Installs all of the PowerPoint program files including PowerPoint Help, Graphic filters, Templates, Clip Art, the PowerPoint Viewer, and the Genigraphics Driver. You need approximately 14 MB of hard disk space to install PowerPoint completely.

Custom Installation   Lets you choose which PowerPoint options to install. Disk space requirements vary depending on the options you choose. As you choose the PowerPoint options you want to install, Setup tells you how much disk space is needed to successfully complete installation. Dictionaries, Graphics Import Filters, Templates, and Clip Art have option buttons that allow you to customize your installation.

PowerPoint Setup on your hard disk

1   If Windows is not currently running, type **win** at the MS-DOS prompt.

-or-

If Windows is running, close all open applications.

2   Insert the PowerPoint Setup disk (Disk 1) in drive A (or B if you are using the B drive).

3   From the Program Manager File menu, choose Run.

The Run dialog box appears.

*Type **a:setup** here*

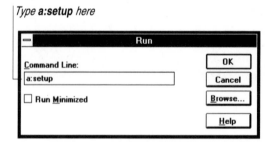

4 Type **a:setup** (or **b:setup** if using the B drive) and click the OK button or press ENTER.

A Welcome dialog box appears and asks you to close all open applications.

Note Click the Help button for information on closing open applications.

5 Click the Continue button to continue Setup.

The Name and Organization Information dialog box appears.

6 Type your name in the Name box to personalize your copy of PowerPoint. (If applicable, press TAB and type your company name in the Organization box.)

7 Click the Continue button or press ENTER.

A dialog box appears requesting you to confirm the information you just entered.

8 Click the Confirm button or press ENTER to confirm the information.

-or-

Click the Change button and type the correct information.

After you click the Confirm button, Setup looks for available disk space on your hard drive to install PowerPoint. When disk space is confirmed, the Directory dialog box appears.

TROUBLESHOOTING: **If a dialog box appears telling you PowerPoint is installed**   Follow the dialog box instructions and refer to your PowerPoint Setup documentation for further information on installing PowerPoint over an existing version.

9 Click the Continue button or press ENTER to accept the directory proposed by Setup.

-or-

Press the BACKSPACE key and type a new directory in the Install To box and then click the Continue button or press the ENTER key.

The Microsoft PowerPoint Installation Options dialog box appears.

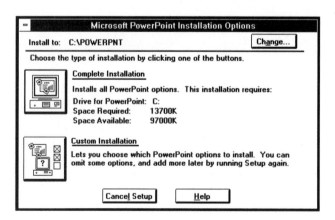

10 Click either the Complete Installation button or the Custom Installation button.

   ■ If you click the Complete Installation button, Setup will begin installing

PowerPoint into the specified directory.

Note   If you click the Complete Installation button, skip steps 11 and 12.

- If you click the Custom Installation button, the Microsoft PowerPoint Custom Installation dialog box appears, allowing you to choose the PowerPoint elements you want to install.

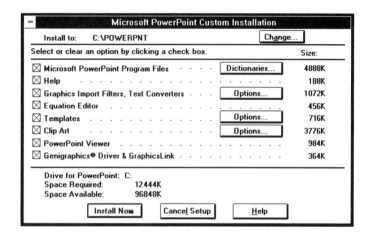

11 Click the appropriate check box or options button to customize your installation.

- Clicking the check box disables the entire option, and Setup won't install it.
- Clicking an Options button allows you to select certain portions of the option you don't want to install.

12 Click the Install Now button to continue Setup from the Microsoft PowerPoint Custom Installation dialog box.

When Setup is complete, a dialog box appears.

13 Click the Continue button or press ENTER.

Setup creates the Microsoft PowerPoint program group and Microsoft PowerPoint, PowerPoint Viewer, and GraphicsLink icons.

After you have installed PowerPoint, you can run Setup at any time to add new features or modify the PowerPoint files already installed.

TrueType Fonts Installed with PowerPoint

PowerPoint installs 22 TrueType fonts when you run Setup. These TrueType fonts (a type of outline font) are stored as instructions for reproducing the shape of each character. TrueType fonts are scaled to create smooth bitmapped characters at any point size. This means your presentation text will look great at any size.

When you run the Setup program, the Font submenu in PowerPoint—which includes all Windows-based applications—displays an overlapping letter "T" to indicate a TrueType font. The TrueType fonts installed with PowerPoint include the following:

- Arial Narrow (plain, italic, bold, bold italic)
- Bookman Old Style (plain, italic, bold, bold italic)
- Book Antiqua (plain, italic, bold, bold italic)
- Century Gothic (plain, italic, bold, bold italic)
- Century Schoolbook (plain, italic, bold, bold italic)
- Monotype Corsiva (italic)
- Monotype Sorts (plain)

Graphic Import Filters Installed with PowerPoint

PowerPoint installs 11 graphic import filters that allow you to import pictures from different applications. PowerPoint uses the import filters when you choose Insert Picture from the Edit menu. The PowerPoint Setup program installs the import filters in a shared location so they can be used by other Microsoft applications. The import filters include the following:

- Macintosh PICT (PCT) Import Filter
- AutoCAD (PLT) Import Filter
- Computer Graphic Metafile (CGM) Import Filter
- Micrografx Designer (DRW) Import Filter
- AutoDesk Drawing Exchange (DXF) Import Filter
- Encapsulated PostScript (EPS) Import Filter
- HP Graphic Language (HGL) Import Filter
- PC Paintbrush (PCX) Import Filter
- Lotus 1-2-3 Graphics (PIC) Import Filter
- Tagged Image File Format (TIF) Import Filter
- WordPerfect Graphics (WPG) Import Filter

Installing and Selecting a Printer

This appendix provides information on installing and setting up a printer for use with Microsoft PowerPoint. In order to print a PowerPoint presentation, the target printer must be properly installed and configured in your Windows 3.1 Control Panel. After the target printer is installed, you can set PowerPoint print and slide options that allow you to print your presentation in the format of your choice.

Installing a New Printer

If your printer was not installed when you installed Microsoft Windows 3.1 or if you purchased a new printer, you can install a printer using one of two methods:

Setup Program   The Setup program you used to install Microsoft Windows 3.1 includes a printer setup section. You can run Windows Setup at any time to install a new printer(s). Refer to your Windows 3.1 Setup documentation for further information on setting up a printer.

Control Panel   The Control Panel is a Windows utility application that can run simultaneously with PowerPoint. Using the Control Panel is the recommended way to install a new printer, because printer changes can be made without closing your PowerPoint application.

The following basic procedures explain how to access the Control Panel, open the Printers dialog box to make changes, and open the Connect dialog box.

Open the Control Panel from PowerPoint

1   Hold down the ALT key and press the TAB key repeatedly until the Program Manager icon appears, and then release the ALT key.

-or-

Hold down the CTRL key and press the ESC key to get the Task List dialog box. Select Program Manager and click the Switch To button.

2   From the Main program group, double-click the Control Panel icon.

The Control Panel window appears, showing various Windows environment settings that can be changed or modified (for example, date and time, screen colors, fonts, mouse actions, and desktop operations).

Your Control Panel window might look similar to the following illustration:

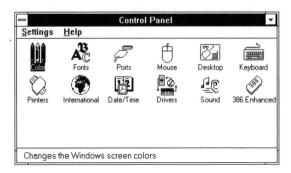

Install a new printer

Use the Printers dialog box in the Control Panel to install and configure a new printer.

1 From the Control Panel, double-click the Printers icon.

The Printers dialog box appears.

The Printers dialog box lists the printers installed on your system and the one which is currently the default printer.

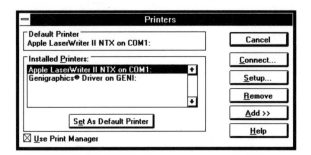

2 Click the Add button to expand the dialog box.

The Printers dialog box should now look similar to the following illustration:

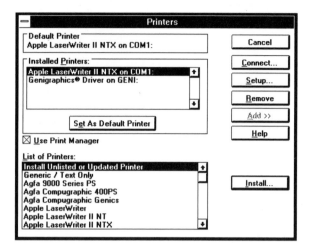

3   To install a printer, select the printer from the List of Printers box and click the Install button.

Note   If the Install Driver dialog box appears, insert the appropriate Microsoft Windows 3.1 disk to install the appropriate printer driver file.

The new printer appears in the Installed Printers box. To delete a printer from the List of Printers box, select the printer(s) and click the Remove button.

Configure a printer

Whenever you install a new printer and its appropriate printer driver file, you need to configure the printer by assigning it to a printer port in the Connect dialog box.

1   From the Printers dialog box, click the Connect button.

The Connect dialog box appears. The Ports box lists the printer ports available to connect your computer with your printer.

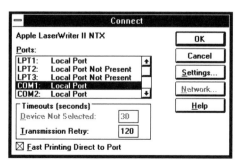

2   Select the appropriate port and click the OK button.

Printer port changes made in the Control Panel Connect dialog box change the settings in the PowerPoint Print Setup dialog box.

One port can have more than one printer assigned to it. You can set up this configuration by selecting the printer(s) and assigning the same port for each printer (repeat the first three steps in this section). To determine which port is active for which printer, check the Print Setup dialog box in the PowerPoint File menu.

Close the dialog boxes and exit the Control Panel

Use the following procedure to close the dialog boxes and return to your PowerPoint presentation window. For a complete explanation of printer installation, port selection, and making printers active, see your Windows documentation.

1   To apply the changes you've made in the Connect dialog box, click the OK button.

-or-

To cancel changes made, click the Cancel button.

2   Click the Close button to close the Printers dialog box.

3   Close the Control Panel by double-clicking on the Control-menu box.

Selecting a Printer

The printer you select controls more than just the final printout; it controls the fonts and formats of your PowerPoint presentation. Printers differ in their abilities to use character formats, spacing, alignment, graphics, and fonts. However, PowerPoint users no longer have to be concerned about target and draft printers. The introduction of TrueType fonts allows PowerPoint to format text independently of the printer, and the new drawing capabilities allow automatic slide scaling to fit any printer if the slide size does not fit the paper.

The printer you select remains selected for all PowerPoint presentations until you manually change it to another printer by changing the Print Setup dialog box settings.

If you have more than one printer installed on your computer, select the Print Setup command from the PowerPoint File menu and select the printer you want PowerPoint to use.

Select a printer in PowerPoint

1   From the File menu, choose Print Setup.

The Print Setup dialog box appears, showing two options boxes.

- The top option box displays the printer for Slides.
- The bottom option box displays the printer for Notes, Handouts, and Outline.

The dialog box that appears on your screen might be different than the one shown in the following illustration:

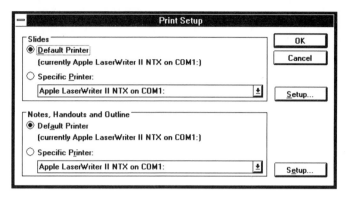

2   If the printer you want is not listed as the default or specific printer, click the down arrow next to the Specific Printer box to view the available printers installed on your system.

3   Select the printer you want PowerPoint to use.

4   Click the OK button.

Changing Print Setup Options

On certain printers you can change the settings for paper orientation, paper size, and paper source. If these options are available on your printer, the default settings can be set for each PowerPoint presentation independently. Use the Print Setup command to change these options.

Print setup settings

You can set the page orientation, paper size, and paper source for all PowerPoint presentations using the following procedure:

1   From the File menu, select Print Setup.

The Print Setup dialog box appears.

2   Click the Setup button from the appropriate print option box (this depends on what view your presentation will be printed in: Slides or Notes, Handouts, and Outline).

A setup dialog box appears.

New Features in Microsoft PowerPoint

PowerPoint version 3 has many new features, as well as improved ones, that make it easier for you to get great results. PowerPoint version 3 is designed specifically for Windows 3.1, which enables new technologies like TrueType fonts and Object Linking and Embedding to be used by PowerPoint. There are improvements in text handling, outlining, graphing and drawing, masters and templates, printing, on-screen slide shows, and exchanging files between platforms.

The following tables list the features that are new in Microsoft PowerPoint version 3, along with the lesson in this book in which you can learn about each feature.

New Ease-of-Use Features

To learn how to	See
Quickly change to Slide and Notes view with buttons	Lesson 1, "Changing Views"
Quickly create a new slide with a button	Lesson 1, "Creating a New Slide in Slide View"
Change the view scale with Toolbar button	Lesson 1, "Changing View Scale"
Change the home view with a Toolbar button	Lesson 1, "Changing View Scale"
Set and change font size, bold, italic, shadow, and bullet text attributes with Toolbar buttons	Lesson 2, "Changing Text Attributes"
Pick Up/Apply Color Scheme with Toolbar buttons	Lesson 6, "Using a Color Scheme"
Set and change line, fill, and shadow object attributes with Toolbar buttons	Lesson 7, "Modifying Object Attributes"
Open a Macintosh PowerPoint 3 presentation	Appendix D, "Presentations on the Go"

New Text and Outlining Features

To learn how to	See
Outline text in all views	Lesson 3, "Outlining Your Ideas"
Edit text in Outline view	Lesson 3, "Edit and Rearranging in Outline View"
Demote and promote text with Toolbar buttons	Lesson 3, "Edit and Rearranging in Outline View"
Move text up and down with Toolbar buttons	Lesson 3, "Edit and Rearranging in Outline View"
Drag text in all views	Lesson 3, "Edit and Rearranging in Outline View"
Save and outline in Rich Text Format	Lesson 3, "Saving an Outline"
Import outlines from other formats (RTF, TXT, and DOC)	Lesson 3, "Inserting an Outline"
Create text label or word processing text with the Text tool	Lesson 4, "Adding Text"
Turn on automatic bullets in text bodies	Lesson 4, "Adding Text"
Adjust text baseline and line spacing	Lesson 4, "Adjusting Text"
Change text object attributes with Fit Text	Lesson 4, "Adjusting Text"
Save a presentation with embeddable TrueType fonts	Appendix D, "Presentations on the Go"

New Master and Template Features

To learn how to	See
Access all masters with view buttons	Lesson 5, "Understanding PowerPoint Masters"
Control title and body format, background items, and color scheme with Follow Master	Lesson 5, "Following the Master"
Reset slides with Reapply Master	Lesson 5, "Following the Master"
Apply templates using the Apply Template command	Lesson 5, "Understanding and Applying Templates"
Use any presentation as a template or one of 160 preformatted templates	Lesson 5, "Changing Masters and Applying Templates"

New Drawing and Object Features

To learn how to	See
Pick up and apply style with Toolbar buttons	Lesson 4, "Formatting Text"
Draw one of 24 shapes with the Shapes tool	Lesson 7, "Working with Objects"
Change or adjust an object's shape	Lesson 7, "Working with Objects"
Draw and edit arcs	Lesson 7, "Drawing and Editing an Arc"
Draw and edit freeform objects	Lesson 7, "Drawing and Editing a Freeform Object"
Rotate or flip objects	Lesson 7, "Rotating and Flipping Objects"
Group, ungroup, or regroup objects	Lesson 7, "Grouping and Ungrouping Objects"
Copy and paste clip art from a collection of over 500	Lesson 11, "Adding Clip Art"
Copy and paste a timesaver diagram	Lesson 11, "Using Timesavers"
Insert a picture	Lesson 11, "Inserting a Picture"
Recolor pictures	Lesson 11, "Recoloring a Picture"
Scale (at 100% of original) or crop pictures to size	Lesson 11, "Scaling Objects"
Link objects to source documents	Lesson 12, "Linking a Picture"

New Graph Features

To learn how to	See
Create graphs with the Graph tool on the Tool Palette	Lesson 8, "Starting Graph"
Graph colors follow the PowerPoint color scheme	Lesson 8, "Working with Graph Basics"

New Printing Features

To learn how to	See
Print slides, notes, and handouts	Lesson 13, "Printing Slides, Notes, Handouts and Outlines"
Print WYSIWYG outlines	Lesson 13, "Printing Slides, Notes, Handouts and Outlines"
Print color presentations in gray-scale or black and white	Lesson 13, "Printing Slides, Notes, Handouts and Outlines"
Print your presentation with automatic scaling to fit your screen or printed page	Lesson 13, "Printing Slides, Notes, Handouts and Outlines"
Print build slides separately	Lesson 15, "Setting Build Slides for a Slide Show"

New Slide Show Features

To learn how to	See
Quickly present a Slide Show with the Slide Show Toolbar button	Lesson 15, "Freehand Drawing in Slide Show"
Create transition effects between slides	Lesson 15, "Setting Slide Transitions and Timings"
Create build slide effects	Lesson 15, "Setting Build Slides for a Slide Show"
Draw freehand information during an on-screen Slide Show	Lesson 15, "Freehand Drawing in Slide Show"
Rehearse and set slide show timings	Lesson 15, "Setting Slide Transitions and Timings"
Start a slide show with the PowerPoint Viewer	Lesson 15, "Using the PowerPoint Viewer"

Presentations on the Go

With PowerPoint, you can open, change, or show electronic presentations on different Windows and Apple Macintosh computers. Whether you're travelling across the country or to the office, you can work on your presentation up to the very last minute.

Opening Presentations on Different Windows 3.1 Systems

PowerPoint presentations created on a computer with one set of fonts might look different when opened on another computer. With PowerPoint and Windows 3.1, you can embed a presentation's fonts into a presentation, and then when you move from one computer to another, the embedded fonts are included in your presentation and are always available when you work or show your presentation.

Which fonts can be embedded?

PowerPoint will let you embed only those fonts electronically marked by the font manufacturer as able to be "embedded and copied without restriction." These include any of the 22 TrueType fonts supplied with Microsoft PowerPoint. If a font can't be embedded, PowerPoint will let you know.

The TrueType fonts that are supplied with Windows 3.1 are expected to be available on all computers running Windows 3.1, so these fonts aren't embedded by PowerPoint.

When to embed fonts

Embed a font only when you think that the fonts will not be available on the system you'll be using. Including embedded fonts in your presentation adds to the file size. For example, if you embed Century Schoolbook Bold, the file size of your presentation will increase by about 60K. Remember that the different font styles— plain, italic, bold and bold italic— are all separate fonts. Each font style increases the file size.

How to embed fonts

1 Open the PowerPoint presentation in which you want to embed fonts.

2 Be sure the presentation includes embeddable fonts.

3 From the File menu, choose Save As.

   The Save As dialog box appears.

4 In the File Name box, type in a file name.

5 Click the With Fonts check box.

The Save As dialog box should look similar to the following illustration:

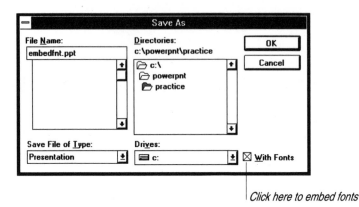

Click here to embed fonts

6 Click the OK button.

Opening Presentations on Different Platforms

You can open Macintosh PowerPoint version 3 presentations in Windows. If you have a Macintosh PowerPoint 2 presentation, you'll have to convert the presentation to version 3 before converting to Windows. Similarly, you can open Windows PowerPoint version 3 presentations on the Apple Macintosh with PowerPoint version 3 for the Macintosh. If you don't have the PowerPoint application, you can view presentations on either platform with the PowerPoint Viewer.

Exchange platforms

Opening presentations on either platform requires that you move the presentation to the platform in which you want to open the file. Two simple ways to move a presentation between platforms are to use a network where Apple Macintosh computers and Windows-based computers are connected or a file exchange application. No special translators are needed to exchange a presentation between platforms. Use the default translator that comes with the file exchange application.

Open Macintosh presentations in Windows

1 From the File menu, choose Open.

The Open dialog box appears.

2 In the Drive box, click the drop-down arrow and select a disk or network drive with the Macintosh PowerPoint version 3 presentation.

3   In the List Files of Type box, click the drop-down arrow and select All Files (*.*).

Macintosh files do not have a *.PPT extension. Only the first eight characters of the Macintosh file name are used in Windows. For example, a Macintosh presentation with the name "Mac PowerPoint 3" appears as "macpower.poi" in the Open dialog box.

4   Select the Macintosh presentation.

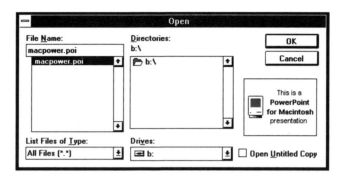

5   Click the OK button.

A dialog box appears.

6   Click the Continue button to translate the Macintosh file and open as an untitled presentation.

Open Windows presentations on the Macintosh

Follow the same general steps in the previous section "Opening Macintosh presentations in Windows" to open a Windows PowerPoint 3 presentation on the Apple Macintosh.

List of Practice Files

You'll find the practice files on the Practice File disk included with this book. Be sure to use the installation program to copy the entire PRACTICE directory to your hard drive. The following files are in the PRACTICE directory:

CO-WORKR.PPT	LESSON11.PPT	SHOWLIST.LST
LESSON02.PPT	LESSON12.PPT	SLDSHOW1.PPT
LESSON03.PPT	LESSON13.PPT	SLDSHOW2.PPT
LESSON04.PPT	LESSON14.PPT	TEMPLT05.PPT
LESSON05.PPT	LESSON15.PPT	
LESSON06.PPT	LINKCHRT.XLC	
LESSON07.PPT	LOGO1.TIF	
LESSON08.PPT	LOGO2.TIF	
LESSON09.PPT	OUTLINE.DOC	
LESSON10.PPT	SHEET09.XLS	

The following table lists the practice files you will use in each lesson. The name you will use to rename the practice file appears in the last column.

In this lesson	Open this file	To create or review this presentation
Lesson 1, "Creating a New Presentation"	New Presentation (empty presentation)	BGPROCES.PPT
Lesson 2, "Working with an Existing Presentation"	LESSON02.PPT CO-WORKR.PPT	BGBASICS.PPT
Lesson 3, "Outlining Your Ideas"	LESSON03.PPT OUTLINE.DOC	BGOUTLN.PPT BGOUTRTF.RTF
Lesson 4, "Adding and Modifying Text"	LESSON04.PPT	BGTEXT.PPT
Lesson 5, "Changing Masters and Applying Templates"	LESSON05.PPT TEMPLT05.PPT	BGMASTER.PPT

In this lesson	Open this file	To create or review this presentation
Lesson 6, "Using a Color Scheme"	LESSON06.PPT	BGCOLOR.PPT
Lesson 7, "Drawing and Modifying Objects"	LESSON07.PPT	BGOBJECT.PPT
Lesson 8, "Creating a Graph"	LESSON08.PPT	BGGRAPH.PPT
Lesson 9, "Editing Graph Data "	LESSON09.PPT SHEET09.XLS	BGEDTGRP.PPT
Lesson 10, "Formatting a Graph"	LESSON10.PPT	BGFMTGPH.PPT
Lesson 11, "Inserting Information into PowerPoint"	LESSON11.PPT LOGO1.TIF LOGO2.TIF	BGINSERT.PPT
Lesson 12, "Linking Information with Other Applications"	LESSON12.PPT LINKCHRT.XLC	BGLINK.PPT
Lesson 13, "Setting Up Your Slides and Printing"	LESSON13.PPT	BGPRNTNG.PPT
Lesson 14, "Producing 35mm Slides"	LESSON14.PPT	BGGENI.PPT
Lesson 15, "Producing an Electronic Presentation"	LESSON15.PPT SLDSHOW1.PPT SLDSHOW2.PPT SHOWLIST.LST	BGSLDSHO.PPT

Glossary

Accent colors The last three colors in the color scheme. These colors are designed to work as the colors for secondary features on the slide.

active cell The currently selected cell of a datasheet, indicated by a heavy border.

adjustment handle A fifth selection handle, usually not in the corner of the selection box. Depending on the shape of the object, you can adjust its features by dragging this handle.

anchor point The point that remains stable as the text grows and shrinks during editing; for example, a top anchor point with a left text alignment allows the text to grow right and down as it normally would when you type. A top center anchor point would allow the text to grow left, right, and down.

application A piece of software, like Microsoft PowerPoint or Microsoft Excel.

application Control menu A menu that includes commands with which you can control the size and position of the PowerPoint window. If you want to display the application Control-menu box with keys, press ALT+SPACEBAR.

attributes The features of an object, such as color, shadow and pattern.

arrow keys The UP ARROW, DOWN ARROW, LEFT ARROW, and RIGHT ARROW keys, used to move the insertion point or select from a menu or list of options.

automatic link A link to information that is updated whenever the information is changed. With an automatic link, PowerPoint updates the information when the original has changed.

axis A line that serves as a major reference for plotting data in a graph.

Background color The first color in the color scheme. The background color is the underlying color of a slide. All colors added to your presentation are added over the background color. To change the background color, change the first color of the color scheme.

background items Objects you add to the master slide so they will appear on the slides in a presentation. *Any object* on the Masters other than the Title or Body objects is considered a background item.

Body object The body on a slide.

body placeholder   The empty Body object that appears on a new slide.

body style   A Follow Master item (from the Slide menu) which can be turned on or off to follow the Master Body style.

build   A bullet point that has been given a build time setting for a slide show.

build slide   A progressive disclosure slide seen during Slide Show. This is a slide that starts with the first major bullet point and then progressively shows the other major bullet points of that slide.

bullet   A mark, usually a round or square dot, used to emphasize or distinguish items in a list.

cell   One rectangle of the datasheet where you enter data.

chart window   The window within Graph that contains the sample graph in which your data appears in graph form as you enter it into the Datasheet.

click   To press and release a mouse button in one nonstop motion.

Clipboard   A temporary storage area for cut or copied text or graphics. You can cut or copy contents from any application, like PowerPoint or Word, to the Clipboard and then paste them into any application. The Clipboard holds only one cut or copied piece of information at a time.

Color Scheme   The basic set of eight colors provided for any slide. The color scheme consists of a Background color, a color for Lines and Text, and six Remaining colors balanced to provide a professional look to your presentation. Color schemes can be applied to slides, and to notes pages.

column control box   The box to the left of the column heading. Click this box to select a column; double-click to exclude or include the data in the graph.

column heading   The left column of the datasheet where column labels are entered.

control handle   The black square that appears at each vertex of arcs and freeform objects when editing. Edit these forms by selecting and dragging the control handle.

Control Panel   The Microsoft Windows application that adjusts operations and formats, such as date, time, screen color, fonts, and printer settings. The settings affect both Windows and PowerPoint.

crop   To trim away the parts of a graphic or picture you don't want to display.

cut   To remove selected text or graphics from a slide so you can place it in another slide, presentation, or application. The information cut is placed on the Clipboard and stays there until another piece of information is cut or copied.

data marker A bar, shape, dot, or symbol that marks a single data point or value. Related markers in a graph make up a data series. Data markers are the bars, columns, areas, pies, lines, and xy scatter points that make up a graph.

data point A single cell item, representing a single item in a data series.

data series A row or column of a datasheet used to draw one or more data markers on a graph.

datasheet window The window within Graph that contains the sample datasheet in which you enter your data.

defaults Predefined settings such as slide size, slide orientation, color settings, and fonts. Use appropriate dialog boxes and master views to change defaults.

default presentation The presentation PowerPoint uses as a template when you don't specify another. Any presentation can be chosen to be the default template.

dialog box A box that displays available command options to review or change.

directories Subdivisions of a disk that work like a filing system to help organize your files. You can create directories from the Windows File Manager.

double lines Indicate separate data series between rows and columns.

drag To hold down the mouse button while moving the mouse.

edit To add, delete, or change text, objects, and graphics.

embedding Storing information inside your PowerPoint presentation that was created using an embedded application. The information that was not a part of your presentation before embedding now becomes a part of your presentation.

file A presentation that has been created and saved under a unique file name. PowerPoint stores all presentations as files.

Fills color The fifth color in the color scheme. The Fills color is a good color to use to fill objects. This color contrasts with the Background and Lines and Text colors.

font The general shapes for a set of characters. Each font has a name with which you can select the font and apply it to text.

frame The line that forms the object. The four lines of a rectangle are its frame the three lines of a triangle are its frame, etc. You can change the style of the frame by changing the line style.

four-headed arrow   The pointer you use to move text lines and paragraphs around the text body.

graph text   The text that describes items or data in a graph.

Graph tool   The tool on the Tool Palette that allows you to access PowerPoint Graph. Select the Graph tool and draw a box on the slide where you want to place the graph.

graph window   The window in which you work with Graph. Similar to the PowerPoint window.

grid   An invisible network of lines that covers the slide. The grid automatically aligns objects to the nearest intersection of the grid.

grid lines   Optional lines that extend from the tick marks on an axis across the plot area to make it easier to view data values.

group   A multiple selection that is treated as a single object by using the Group command in the Arrange menu.

guides   Two straightedges, one horizontal and one vertical, used for visually aligning objects. Objects can be aligned at the corner or the center depending upon which is closer.

icon   A graphical representation of a file-level object (for example, a disk drive, a directory, an application, or other object that you can select and open).

landscape   A term used to refer to horizontal page orientation; opposite of portrait orientation.

legend   The key that identifies the patterns, colors, or symbols associated with the markers of a data series and shows the data series name that corresponds to each marker.

levels   The different paragraph indentations at which paragraphs appear in an outline.

Lines and Text color   The second color in the color scheme that contrasts with the background color for writing text and drawing lines on the slide. Together with the Background color, the Lines and Text color sets the tone for the presentation.

linking   Using information within your presentation that is stored outside your presentation. The information remains "attached" to the original source while you work on it in your PowerPoint presentation. Linked information automatically updates to the information source file and application.

manual link   A link to information that is updated only by the user.

Master Body   The formatted body on the Slide Master. The Master Body controls the font, color, size, and alignment of the body object as well as the placement on the slide.

Master Title   The formatted title on the Slide Master. The Master Title controls the font, color, size, and alignment of the title text as well as the object attributes (fill, line, and shadow), shape, and placement on the slide.

menu   A list of commands that drop down from the menu bar. The menu bar displays across the top of the application window and lists the menu names (for example, File and Edit).

Move Up/Move Down   To move a paragraph up is to exchange it with the one above. To move a paragraph down is to exchange it with the one below.

multiple selection   Selecting more than one object using the SHIFT+click method or by dragging the selection rectangle. When you flip, rotate, or resize a multiple selection, all objects in the multiple selection react independently.

object   A single component of your drawing. Objects can be drawn from the Tool Palette, which includes ovals, rectangles, freeform shapes, arcs, and graphs.

Other colors   Non-scheme colors you can use for special purposes. Every color menu has an "Other Color" choice on it so you can choose a special color. Your "Other Colors" will not automatically change when you choose a different color scheme for a presentation.

outlining functions   Promoting and demoting paragraphs to different levels in the outline and moving them up and down within your presentation. These functions work in any PowerPoint view.

paste   To insert cut or copied text or graphics into a presentation from the Clipboard.

paste special   To insert cut or copied text or graphics with a special format (for example, BMP and RTF for graphics and text, respectively).

picture   An image from another application. A picture has object properties. You can resize it, move it, and recolor it; and some pictures can be ungrouped into component objects. When ungrouping a picture, you separate it into PowerPoint objects that when regrouped become a PowerPoint object (not a picture).

plot area   The area where Graph plots your data. It includes the axes and all markers that represent data points.

portrait   A term used to refer to vertical page orientation; opposite of landscape orientation.

promote/demote To move text line(s) or paragraph(s) out or in a level in the outline. Usually, when you promote text, it moves to the left; when you demote text, it moves to the right.

regular shape A perfectly proportioned shape that can be inscribed within a square. You can draw regular shapes by using the SHIFT key. The following shapes can be made regular by using the SHIFT key: circle, square, diamond, cross, star, hexagon, equilateral triangle, and octagon.

Remaining colors The six additional colors in the color scheme. Color scheme numbers three through eight.

resize handle The black square at each corner of a selected object. Dragging a resize handle resizes an object.

row control box The box above a row heading. Click this box to select a row; double-click to exclude or include the data in the graph.

row heading The top row of the datasheet where row labels are entered.

ruler A graphical bar displayed across the top of a Text object. From the ruler you can set tabs and indents to any Text object.

scale To change an object's size by reducing or enlarging it by a constant percentage.

scroll bar A graphical device for moving vertically and horizontally through a presentation slide with the pointer. Scroll bars are located along the right and bottom edges of the presentation window.

selection box The "fuzzy" outline around an object that indicates it is selected. Selecting and dragging the selection box moves the object.

series names The names that identify each row or column of data.

Shadows color The third color in the color scheme and the first Remaining color (see Remaining colors). PowerPoint applies the Shadows color to a shadowed object. The color is often a darker shade of the Background color.

shape The form of an object, such as rectangle, circle or square. The shape is also an attribute because you can change the object's shape without redrawing the object. Arcs, freeforms, and lines are not considered shapes.

Slide Changer A tool located on the lower left side of the presentation window used to move from slide to slide or notes page to notes page. Click the up arrow or down arrow, drag the lever, or click above or below the lever to change slide or notes page.

slide Control menu A menu with commands that control a document window's size and position. To display the slide Control-menu box with keys, press ALT+HYPHEN.

source   The document that contains the original information; the document to which you are linking.

stacking   The placement of objects one on top of another.

template   A presentation whose format and color scheme you apply to another presentation. There are 160 professionally designed templates (four categories of 40 templates each) that come with PowerPoint, but *any* template can be used.

text attributes   Characteristics of text, including font, type size, style, color, etc. Changing text attributes can occur before or after you have typed the text.

text editing buttons   Buttons on the Toolbar used to change the attributes of text, including font size, bold, italic, underline, shadow, and bullet.

tick-mark   A small line that intersects an axis and marks off a category, scale, or data series. The tick mark label identifies the tick mark.

tick-mark labels   The names that appear along the horizontal axis of an area, column, line graph or along the vertical axis of a bar graph. When data series are in rows, the tick-mark labels are the column labels. When data series are in columns, the tick-mark labels are the row labels.

timings   The amount of time a slide stays on the screen during Slide Show. Each slide can have a different timing.

Title object   The title on the slide.

title placeholder   The empty Title object that appears on a new slide.

title style   A Follow Master command item (from the Slide menu), which can be turned on or off to follow the Master Title style.

Title Text color   The fourth color in the color scheme. This color, like the Lines and Text color, contrasts with the Background color.

Toolbar   The graphical bar across the top of the presentation window with buttons that perform some of the common commands in PowerPoint. The Toolbar changes in PowerPoint depending on the view, except for Slide and Notes view, which uses the same Toolbar.

Tool Palette   The graphical bar on the left side of the PowerPoint window. The Tool Palette holds the drawing tools, the Graph tool, and the Slide Changer.

transitions   The effects that move one slide off the screen and the next slide on during Slide Show. Each slide can have its own transition effect.

vertex/vertices   The point(s) where two straight lines meet.

view   A display that shows a presentation in a certain way. PowerPoint has four views—Slide, Outline, Notes and Handout.

window   A rectangular area on your screen in which you view and work on presentations.

Index

Symbols